Conversations with Silence

Conversations with Silence

Rosetta Stone of the Soul

SALLY LONGLEY

Foreword by Trevor Hudson

CASCADE *Books* · Eugene, Oregon

CONVERSATIONS WITH SILENCE
Rosetta Stone of the Soul

Cascade Books
An Imprint of Wipf and Stock Publishers
199 W. 8th Ave., Suite 3
Eugene, OR 97401

www.wipfandstock.com

PAPERBACK ISBN: 978-1-7252-7775-5
HARDCOVER ISBN: 978-1-7252-7776-2
EBOOK ISBN: 978-1-7252-7777-9

Cataloguing-in-Publication data:

Names: Longley, Sally, author. | Hudson, Trevor, 1951–, foreword writer

Title: Conversations with silence : Rosetta Stone of the soul / Sally Longley : foreword by Trevor Hudson.

Description: Eugene, OR: Cascade Books, 2021 | Includes bibliographical references.

Identifiers: ISBN 978-1-7252-7775-5 (paperback) | ISBN 978-1-7252-7776-2 (hardcover) | ISBN 978-1-7252-7777-9 (ebook)

Subjects: LCSH: Silence—Religious aspects—Christianity | Spiritual life | Silence—Religious aspects

Classification: BV4509.5 L66 2020 (paperback) | BV4509.5 (ebook)

12/17/20

To our two remarkable adult children, Philip and Claire, who have both taught me so much about how to listen and ways of seeing. Thank you for the unspeakable joy you give. And to Jim, my companion and anam chara always.

Contents

Permissions

Foreword

Several years ago, a dear friend and mentor wrote, "The one journey that ultimately matters is the journey into the place of stillness deep within oneself."[1] These words scorched their way into my seeking heart when I first read them in the early eighties. They set on fire within its furnace an intense longing to engage this still space where those further along the Way told me the ever-present Mystery that we call God would encounter me. In this beautifully written book, another veteran of the Spirit came alongside me on my pilgrimage into silence and fanned this desire into even greater flame. Let me share how Sally Longley, the author of the book you are holding, did this for me.

Throughout her book, Sally helps the reader to engage "the worlds of silences." On my recent eight-day retreat, my Jesuit guide said to me, "Trevor, insight is the consolation prize. Encounter is first prize." As I read this book, his words came back to me. In these pages we are not so much given loads of information *about* silence; rather, we are invited into an encounter *with* silence. Certainly, this happened for me in my reading. Again, and again, I needed to pause, in quietness and silence, so I could ponder the invitations of the divine Spirit tucked away in the book's images and metaphors. Wondering how to respond faithfully to them within my own life whets my appetite for the ongoing engagement with silence.

There are several ways in which Sally helpfully facilitates this engagement for the reader. Let me mention just three. First, by sharing her different experiences of encountering silence, she points us towards gateways through which we can enter the silence. She generously describes her own moments of silent encounter as she faces the wounds of her own

---

1. Gordon Cosby wrote these words in his Foreword to O'Connor, *Search for Silence*, 11.

shadow within a long retreat, enjoys the hospitality and welcome of desert hermits, gives voice to those who have been traumatized and silenced by oppressive structures, embraces the small pauses that come her way in her everyday life, notices the visual and physical spaces around her, and in many other ways. She trusts that what has been most personal on her own journey will echo in our experiences. It resonated for me and I am sure will also do so for you.

Then, Sally encourages our engagement with silence by drawing us into a deeper reflection of our own experiences of silence. In my early years of pastoral ministry, my supervisor would constantly say, "We don't learn from experience, we learn when we reflect on experience." By reflecting at depth on Sally's own personal encounters with silence, we learn from her the value of pondering our own. Every day "little solitudes" and "little silences" come our way, providing us with the necessary space to listen to what is happening around and within us. These surprising moments, as we are reminded here, are already "content-filled." They do not need to be filled with anything else! Taking the time to reflect upon them in the hurly-burly of our everyday lives, and to listen to the Divine Whisper, will be profoundly transformative.

Lastly, Sally brings to her writing a contagious trust that the Great Love at the heart of the universe will meet us in the silence. This is the good news that she has come to *know*. She writes as a first-hand witness to this silent encounter with the Divine Mystery in the present moment. This knowing has come through her own experiences of wonder, lostness, struggle, seeking, disorientation, seeking, and finding, which characterize the lives of all those who seek God in the silence. As such, she stands with integrity among all those mostly hidden women and men who throughout the ages have kept alive what has been called "the work of silence."

There are at least two ways in which this book can be read. One is to read it through for the sake of the personal nourishment and inspiration that comes from being in the company of a seasoned adventurer who has herself traversed some of the landscapes of silence. This could be the way you read the book for the first time. The other possibility is to read the book slowly, pausing to reflect, and to engage the suggested exercises that will help you to participate in the silence. This second way of reading will guide you on that arduous, life-transforming, and critical journey to the place of stillness deep within you, where the Eternal One waits to meet you. While you may often be tempted to give up on this journey, the words written here will encourage you to keep going.

I could write so much more in gratitude for this book. Looking at the bibliography, we can see that this book is the distillation of many years of rigorous academic study. It truly is a gift of grace, given with no strings attached. At no stage while reading did I sense the author trying to convert me to silence. While I heard in her writing voice the distinctive accent of a faithful Christ-follower, there is no proselytizing. Rather, in a warm embrace of other voices from differing cultural and religious backgrounds, there comes to the reader the eternal invitation to be still and to know God. This is the ultimate journey that matters most. Sally is a trusted guide for our next step.

TREVOR HUDSON
Benoni, South Africa, July 2020
Author, teacher, retreat-giver

Acknowledgments

I am grateful to those who accompanied me in the various early stages of this project: Patti Miller, Anthony Reeder, and Fr. Dennis Billy, C.Ss.R. Your guidance and feedback helped set the trajectory for the book. I have received such wise, warm, and generous attentiveness to chapters of my work from Angela Moore, Jim Longley, and Rabbi Howard Avruhm Addison. Thank you for your companionship along the way. I am grateful to Trisha Dale, dear friend and wonderful wordsmith. My deep thanks to Dr. Julie Thorpe, who walked through each chapter with me, a trusted companion trekking through the woods of words. You alert me constantly to the enchanted world of images, the liturgies of trees, and the sounding of my true voice. You have been a gift indeed. And to Trevor Hudson, who graciously accepted to write the foreword for this book, and whose life and work I deeply respect.

1

Rosetta Stone of the Soul

The heavens herald your glory, O God,
and the skies display your handiwork.
Day after day they tell their story,
and night after night they reveal
the depth of their understanding.
Without speech, without words,
without even an audible voice,
their cry echoes through all the world,
and their message reaches the ends of the earth.
(Ps 19:1–4)[1]

Without speech, without word, without even an audible voice, and yet their cry goes out: how do we translate this form of speech? What is the language and vocabulary of such voices that speak out of no sound, out of silence?

---

1. Priests for Equality, *The Inclusive Bible.*

1

One of the most significant archaeological artifacts available to us is the Rosetta Stone, found in 1799 by French Napoleonic troops in Egypt. Created around 196 BCE, the black granodiorite stela has a tripartite inscription carved into it in the three languages of Egyptian hieroglyphics (a script used for important religious documents), Egyptian demotic script (the common script of the day), and ancient Greek (the ruler's language at the time). For hundreds of years, archaeologists had been trying to decipher hieroglyphics, but to no avail. When the stone was found, because the three inscriptions consisted of the same decree, the Greek provided the key to understanding the other ancient languages of hieroglyphics and demotics.

The languages of silence and of the soul can likewise become lost in our own personal histories of chaos, busyness, and lack of attentiveness to our interior selves and to silences. Just as the key to conversation across the languages of hieroglyphics and demotics was the Greek, so the key to conversation with silence and the soul is immersion: immersion into stillness and attentiveness. However, unlike deciphering the Rosetta Stone, learning the languages of silence and the soul comes not through a mechanical translation, but rather through a process of interpersonal dialogue and experience. During the years I lived in South Africa, I began to learn the Setswana language, so I went to live with a Tswana family. Being thoroughly soaked in the family, their culture, their nuanced body language and subtle expressions, I was gently corrected and taught by them. I learned then just how relational a language is. To separate language from relationship empties it of content—deep content.

Saturation in the abode and culture of silence enables us to begin to learn the language of silence, and to have a conversation between our souls and silence. The Rosetta Stone hence becomes a poetic analogy. Stillness and attentiveness unlock the door into the world of silences. As we step into this world of silence, filled with many different silences, and allow ourselves to be immersed in silence, to be steeped in it, corrected by it, and to sense its subtle nuances and gestures, our souls can begin the very personal journey of conversations with silence.

The pre-modern world knew how to read the landscape and soundscape of silence. For Egyptian-born Moses, time in the spacious and silent desert enabled him to notice at the periphery of his vision the small movements of God in a burning bush, to move closer and thus hear the surprising voice of "I AM" speaking to him through this small bush. The prophet Elijah heard God speak to him, not in the wind, earthquake, and fire, but in the voice of "sheer silence" (1 Kgs 19:11–13). The priest Zechariah conversed with an angel who spoke him into silence (Luke 1:18–22). The Hebrew psalmist urges us to "wait in silence" for God's response (Ps 62:5–7), while early Christians interpreted voices of the Spirit as groans or sighs "too deep for words" (Rom 8:26), and understood silence as the sound of awe (Rev 8). The desert mothers and fathers knew the value of the silent wilderness as a place for transformation and transfiguration. For Jesus, the silence of the desert opened up a landscape where he was confronted with wild beasts and temptations, as well as being comforted by angels. And to a mystic like John of the Cross, silence was God's first language.

Silence has become an increasing focus of contemporary interest since the landmark work *The World of Silence*, published in 1952 by the German-Swiss Catholic theologian Max Picard. "The silence that precedes speech is the pregnant mother who is delivered of speech by the creative activity of the spirit," he wrote.[2] The Trappist monk Thomas Merton made a similar connection between silence and speech when he observed that "writing and teaching must be fed by silence or they are a waste of time."[3] We need to look to the Rosetta Stone analogy and recover lost languages of God. Entering into silence enables us to become immersed in its culture and language; then we can begin to discern and translate these voices that utter from "no sound."

Studies abound in religious and secular domains, by both scholars and the popular press, examining silence in literary texts and film, spirituality and theology, within conversations and psychological studies, and in forms of art and music. But despite the proliferation of these works, much that is available writes *about* silence, and rarely engages *with* silence as a language that communicates and with which we can dialogue. This is an important distinction. It could be that this proliferation of writing about silence and speaking on behalf of silence risks us not hearing silence speak for itself, and thus we may begin to lose deep knowledge of the language of silence, and become no longer capable of conversing in one of the languages of God.

VENTURING INTO WORLDS OF SILENCE

Over the years of my work as a retreat leader and spiritual director, I have discovered a number of common misconceptions about silence. Some may come to a retreat or inquire how to "de-stress" from work or family life with a sense that silence is monochrome, generally romantic, and that all they need to do is sit in the "peaceful silence" and they will then leave the retreat a new person. This indeed may be the case, but it means they are unprepared for times when they are confronted by difficulties in silence. There is

2. Picard, *World of Silence*, 24.
3. Merton and Montaldo, *Entering the Silence*, 395–96.

much more to the experience of silence, and we may need to be undone first by the work of the Spirit who uses varied silences as the vocabulary of God to call us into a different way of being.

For others, there is great fear: How will I possibly cope? How can I be silent for more than three hours, let alone a whole weekend? What will happen? How can I do without music or having others to talk to all the time? And there are those who have experienced silence but have become bored or numbed to it, or those who have said to me, "I am an extrovert, so silence is not for me!" When I have suggested people read some of the mystics whose lives were embedded in silence, it has seemed that this is a bridge too far in terms of the sometimes-opaque writing styles and concepts. There is a need for something less esoteric, yet accessible to a serious inquirer about silence. My central focus, then, is to introduce some of the extraordinary breadth and depth in the landscapes of silence and, in doing so, to provide an easily available forum for those curious about silence.

There may be times when we find ourselves in silence and on our own, not by choice. It can come due to the sudden departure of a loved one, or as the result of becoming house-bound by illness, or even a global pandemic like COVID-19. Although these can be times of very mixed emotions, they can also be opportunities to learn about ourselves. When we embrace silence, we allow it to teach us about ourselves: What motivates us? What gives us life? What is happening under the many internal layers of noise that is craving to be heard? What is it that we fear? What am I truly longing for? Silence can be like a cataplasm, drawing out the toxins within us, and opening possibilities of healing. Gemma Fiumara, in pointing out that most of us live in cultures where we focus on speaking and neglect listening, suggests that "only when we know how to be silent will that of which we cannot speak begin to tell us something."[4] And in order to hear what that something is, we need to be attentive and still, receptive to this strange world of silence.

Attempting to describe silence is like trying to grasp air: it can be misconstrued as "nothingness" or absence, and yet we are well aware of how our health depends on the content and quality of the air we breathe. Air is central to our lives just as silence is, and our health and personal transformation depend on the quality of silence we engage with. Silence is content-filled and there are as many silences as there are emotions and landscapes. Silences can be angry, calm, brittle, fearful, stunned, affirming, or dreaded. Silence can have spatial and time dimensions: we speak of *entering into* silence or *sitting in* silence, as if it were a room we can move into; or a silence can be long, short, deep, or endless. We also speak of silences as being large

4. Fiumara, *Other Side of Language*, 101.

or of having stretches of silence; we can "travel in silence," and we can reach down into our silence; we can experience empty silence. It can have physical attributes and its own characteristics, such as something we can break, as in "breaking the silence," having weight, such as a "loaded silence," or something that can "fill our ears." As Diarmaid MacCulloch remarks in his *Silence: A Christian History*, "every silence is different and distinctive. Each is charged with the murmurs of the landscape around it, with the personalities of those who have entered it and remain present within it, together with the memories of conversations that have come and gone."[5]

We can be in a silence that is external to ourselves: a silent room, for example. And yet we can be anything but silent internally: we can be full of emotions and noise, clutter and internal conversations with any number of imagined people. To be still and attentive is to bring a gentle settling into our interior worlds—putting aside all that is swirling around within—and to become present and attentive to the silent room, and then slowly that silence begins to soak into us. Then we can begin to notice the nuances and gestures of silence, and of the God who speaks in and through silence. Alternatively, we may be in the middle of a busy street, in a crowded train, or on a hospital ward, and yet be able to find that still point within us: a quiet attentiveness and spaciousness that can experience the gentle voicing of silence within us, and we can converse with this silence. And when we do so, we are conversing with the One who created all things and who speaks through both silence and sound.

It is into the world of silences, with all their nuanced characteristics, language and grammar, that I invite readers to join me as curious explorers. My desire is to enable those who fear silence to delve into ways to engage with silence creatively and to dialogue with its many forms and voices. And for those who have expectations that silence will be an easy cure-all, I hope this will help gain a broader perspective, and nurture the desire to explore further the different landscapes of silence, all in the service of personal and spiritual growth.

As with all adventurers traveling together, it helps to know how we will traverse this world. So before I introduce some of the landscapes we will venture into in each chapter, I will discuss briefly the approaches used.

HOW WILL WE TRAVEL?

Some of the modes of travel we will use are contemplation, imagination, and reflection.

5. MacCulloch, *Silence: A Christian History*, 217.

Contemplation

We may enter silences by means of images, a word, or the five senses. This is known as kataphatic prayer. For some, this form of prayer can then become a gateway into imageless and wordless (or apophatic) prayer of presence. And we may also find ourselves moving along the spectrum between these contemplative modes. For some Africans, African-Americans, and Mennonites, song is a central part of worship and prayer, both privately and corporately, where their contemplative practice sits inside the music. This is in part what Barbara Holmes, the contemporary scholar with a focus on African-American spirituality, refers to in her work *Joy Unspeakable*. One person described her experience to me as being similar to sitting fully submerged in water, with the music flowing over, in, and through her in such a way that the memorized words and music became a dome where silence washed into her heart of hearts. There is also the type of silence that we have become very familiar with—the silence of respect and remembrance, for those who have died. This silence is a universal language, a liturgy of lament globally understood.

Imagination

Another mode by which we can access and engage silence is via the imagination. The creative role of imagination has often been understood as having less value than our reason, and being less worthy. Yet how often has imaginative writing enabled truths to be communicated profoundly, such as in C. S. Lewis's *Narnia* series? And Jesus also taught us a way of imagination by using parables, which can be entered into only via the imagination. Malcolm Guite, the English poet and priest, has described the role of the imagination as a means by which to discover, receive, and be transformed by truths. He suggests that reason alone can get us to the door of a great mystery or truth by enabling us to comprehend *to some extent* what is beyond comprehension. But, he suggests, it is imagination that allows us to apprehend, and I would add *to be apprehended by*, such mysteries. In this way, imagination becomes not a "retreat from reality, but [rather] an essential power with which we engage reality."[6] As we encounter different silences and begin to learn their language, the vocabulary of the soul starts to resonate and as deep calls to deep, silence to soul and soul to silence, a conversation can begin. Such heart-to-heart dialogues may use words, but they also may use sensing, gestures, and simply ways of being with each other. We see partnered ice-skaters

6. Guite, *Faith, Hope and Poetry*, 95.

who have grown into knowing the nuanced language of each other's minute movements, expressions, and emotions, communicating seamlessly in silent harmony, independent yet dependent, initiating and responding. So too, we can learn the subtle language of silence, which becomes a song of the soul, and we glide and dance in a partnership beyond words.

Reflection

Reflection, too, can be a way into silence. In his *Spiritual Exercises*, the sixteenth-century writer Ignatius of Loyola discovered firsthand the importance of reflection upon personal experiences. Born in 1491 in the north of Spain, he sustained a serious injury when fighting the French at Pamplona, when a cannonball shattered his leg. He was returned to his father's castle in Loyola and underwent multiple surgeries. During the long period of recuperation, only two books were available to him: one was on the lives of great saints, and the other on the Gospel texts. Having been known to be a womanizer and once arrested for disorderly behavior in the streets at night, he daydreamed about becoming a romantic hero. But as he read the texts, he started also to daydream on becoming a saint or a disciple of Jesus. He discovered that after a short while, when he reflected on his dreams of romantic heroism, they left him feeling flat, enervated, and empty. However, after imagining becoming a saint and following Jesus, he became aware of feeling energized with a deep sense of life-giving purpose. Ignatius realized that this was a key to the discernment process around the options we have in life-direction as well as smaller, everyday choices. During this time, he also had a vision that led to a dramatic conversion. These experiences changed his desires, and the whole direction of his life.

Ignatius later developed a spiritual practice around reflection, which encompassed reflection on his times of prayer, on imaginative dreaming about life choices, and on daily experiences. Reflection is central to Ignatian spirituality, and alerts us to the significance of the nuanced responses of the body and the spirit, indicating that which is most life-giving and that which is not.

Current Western culture encourages us to collect experiences—travel, sport, recreation, conferences, spiritual experiences, including pilgrimages and retreats. The photographs that result from such experiences are then often put onto social media platforms. But reflection, which takes time and commitment, goes both beyond and deeper than photographs, and tends not to be part of our cluttered, busy, and acquisitive lifestyles. As a result, we become experience-rich but remain transformationally poor. So, then, experience alone can be fascinating, but with reflection on these experiences, paying attention to what is lying deeper underneath and to the movement of the Spirit within, these experiences can become life-changing.

Reflection can turn our lives around, altering the way we live and act in the world, changing our attitudes and values. The resultant inward movements of transformation are then followed by outward movements of action in our social, political, environmental, and economic contexts. The more we invest in the wholeness of our own person, the more we can offer a wholeness into society. Addressing our own growth in wholeness is therefore holy work.

INTERPRETIVE LENSES

All explorers need binoculars, sunglasses, stereoscopes, and telescopes to read landscapes, maps, and the heavens. The interpretive lenses I use include Jewish wisdom and tradition, mystical theology, and feminism, as well as insights from art, poetry, music, and relevant literature.

The wisdom and spiritual traditions of Jewish midrash and exegesis offer valuable insights and, as I stand within the Christian tradition, it is with deep respect that I approach such practices, which offer alternative creative frameworks by which to explore ways of perception and interpretation.

Mystical theology is a branch of theology that opens up ancient spiritual practices such as contemplative prayer. I draw on the insights of several Christian mystics, such as St. John of the Cross, Julian of Norwich, St. Ignatius of Loyola, as well as more modern mystics such as Thomas Merton. Other branches of mysticism I refer to include Egyptian Orthodox and Sufi, where their wisdom has great universal application. Paying attention to these mystics, who have dwelt deeply and for extended periods in the realms of silence, has allowed me to draw on their deep percipience as I reflected on the mysteries of silence. Such people become our guides and spiritual directors,[7] offering comment on our experiences and holding up a mirror for us to see what might be happening more clearly.

Feminism as a lens enables us to hold a corrective lens to much that has been unhealthily patriarchal. The particular place where I did undergraduate studies in theology in the 1980s meant that the whole framework for theological discourse was heavily patriarchal. As I continued in further study and eventually doctoral studies, I was able to engage at depth with far wider paradigms, which challenged and sometimes successfully demolished my early frameworks and enabled me to rethink and recreate positions,

7. Spiritual directors are those with the charism and training to accompany another on their spiritual journey.

which enabled fresh theological vistas that have now gone beyond gender. Some of the feminist authors I refer to include Beverley Lanzetta, Mieke Bal, and Rabbi Jill Hammer. Matthew Fox, one of our modern mystics, suggests what is needed is both the "Divine Feminine" and the "Sacred Masculine" for a healthy perspective.[8] And I would extend this to suggest that we need gendered approaches that are all-inclusive.

Finally, I also seek the companionship of forms of art, music, and poetry, opening up interplays of silence, sound, and visual color and space. They become like the birds and all living creatures that inhabit and give life to the rational, beautiful, and symbolic world of trees. If we walk in the woods where there is no bird call, and no animal movements at all, it is not long before we sense that something very profound is missing. All are needed together for a healthy ecosystem, a wholesomeness, so that when we venture into landscapes we do so in the company of these enlivening guides.

All lenses have both limits and gifts depending upon how we use them. The lenses I have chosen to interpret each experience of silence are used with the intention of providing greater clarity of vision, sometimes using a macro lens for close-up scrutiny, and at other times binoculars that give us hints beyond the horizon.

WHAT LANDSCAPES WILL WE VENTURE INTO?

The chapters are written along the lines of a personal essay, drawing on imaginative elements that at times are similar to magical realism. I draw on my own experiences, some of which are intensely personal, but which may hold some degree of universal application.

There are several ways the chapters may be of use. You could use each chapter as a guided retreat, focusing on any chapter that beckons you. If you are a retreat facilitator, you could adapt the chapters for use over the retreat time. Alternatively, any of the chapters may be helpful reading for those considering going on a silent retreat or for anyone who may be curious about the languages of silence and the soul.

Each chapter begins with recounting an experience, where I invite you to accompany me as I explore one of the landscapes of silence. This is followed by a second section, "Reflection." Here we follow Ignatius's wisdom, looking back on each experience, diving deeper into what was happening. As we look together at what happened, we will draw on the experiences and perspectives of fellow travellers: mystics and artists who have travelled similar paths. In the third section, "Pondering Your Own Experiences," I offer

8. Fox, *Hildegard of Bingen*.

suggestions to enable you to go further into the rich treasures of your own related experiences. The final section, "For Further Engagement," discusses more broadly some of the topics raised in the chapter, which the reader may follow up on if interested.

Each chapter ventures into a different world of silence. In chapters 2 and 3 I explore silences experienced on two very different long retreats.

Chapter 2, "The Eloquence of Shadows," describes a selection of experiences from a week-long silent retreat in a rural area. I look at some of the unusual ways we can converse with silence, as well as hearing silence speak with me through my own shadow, and touch on issues such as identity, ego, self-worth, aging, and loss. It illustrates possible ways the Spirit can use our imagination to enable us to encounter truths that we may find difficult to access simply through reason, and encourages us to trust our imaginations. For those who are drawn to a silent retreat or have questions about how silence can speak, this chapter may be of some interest.

Chapter 3, "Eating Honey with God," takes us into desert experiences. Desert spirituality has a rich history and the wisdom of the desert mothers and fathers offers nourishment for us when we enter unchartered lands within ourselves. The deserts we encounter may be in our environment or they may be internal deserts. In both cases we can experience desolation and consolation. This was certainly the case with me when I was confronted by wild beasts and my ego, and yet too it is also a place where I was ministered to by angels. It is in the furnace of the desert that we are honed and, as the French Jesuit Jean-Pierre de Caussade (1675–1751) described in a letter to a spiritual directee, in the desert we may "make more progress in one month than you would in several years of sweetness and consolation."[9] It is the place where we go when we refuse to let the world shape us into its image, and desire the Spirit to transfigure us into Christ-likeness. Such a desert venture may be something you feel called towards and, if so, this chapter may provide some signposts for the journey.

Chapter 4, "*Tikkun Olam*: Repairing Silence," journeys into a dark form of silence that can come unbidden with trauma. It is the underworld of silence. No book on silence can be complete unless this underside of silence is addressed. There are times when silence is forced upon a person or community due to an imbalance or abuse of power, or it can even be through the ultimate silencing when the person sees their own death as the only solution. *Tikkun olam* refers to the Jewish imperative to engage in acts that heal the world's wounds. In this chapter, I invite the reader to explore midrash with Jewish wisdom as a guide as I retell the apocryphal story of

9. De Caussade, *Abandonment*, Kindle location 7068.

Susanna. She was a survivor of attempted rape, silenced in the experience of the attack itself, in the mock trial that followed, and also in the way artists and biblical commentators have portrayed her through a patriarchal lens over the centuries since. Allowing Susanna to have a voice is my attempt to contribute constructively to the healing of those of us who have been silenced and our voices not heard. And for those who have experienced a form of silencing, this chapter may offer a companion in Susanna.

The next two chapters address possibilities presented to us for encounters with different kinds of silences within our midst, the tiny worlds of silence that are our everyday often-neglected companions in our lives. These experiences can encourage a more attentive awareness of the polyphony of silences in our environments that are like portals into the presence of silence and the Divine.

Chapter 5, "*Selah*: Slivers of Silence," introduces all the small *selahs*—or small moments of silence—that are unnoticed yet rich avenues to enter contemplatively, which can transform the way we live into each day. *Selah* is the word found between stanzas in the Psalms and also in Habakkuk, and is commonly understood to mean a pause. This chapter uses *selah* to name the small pauses we encounter, such as while reading literature or Scripture, shopping in an antiquarian bookstore, or those silences we hear in the music we are listening to. These are all like tiny houses of time that we may enter and sometimes surprisingly find in the voices of such silences the expansive hospitality of God. As usual, silence begins to draw out the poison from within our bodies, and so I grapple with the issues of guilt, trust, and confession; receive gifts of gold through the poetry of Patrick Kavanagh as I choose to enter a tiny silence; and discover what it means to soar on silences in music.

In chapter 6, "*Ma*: Emptiness Full of Possibility," I continue exploring the small landscapes of silence, by opening out the many physical or visual spaces we encounter daily. The concept of *ma* comes from the Japanese aesthetic referring to the spaces between objects, such as in architectural spaces or in an ikebana arrangement. For example, the space between pillars or framed by a gate can itself be a framed visual silence, a contemplative space to enter into. All these spaces are referred to as *ma* and can be found in nature—between branches of a tree, the calm visual space-time between waves, the juggled spaces between a row of sparrows lined up on the edge of a birdbath. There are also the apparent blank spaces within works of art that form the painterly equivalent of silence, or the background of an icon. Some of the issues I dip into include the sense of interior emptiness; the paradox of God's immanence and transcendence; the intimacy, tenderness, and touchability of God; and the role of icons and *ma* in prayer. I also invite you into iconography in all its remarkable multifaceted process, as I notice the ways in which God speaks to me in and through the minutiae of detail. These are spaces full of possibilities and provide accessible entry points into hearing the voices of the Trinity, helping us enter deeper into contemplative living from day to day.

The final chapter, "God Comes to Us in Silence," draws together the threads and takes us forward: in the light of where we have traveled together, how then do we want to live? The contemporary composer Arvo Pärt may have a clue for us. He was reported to have encountered a conductor once, who

> was rushing through one of his works, trying to fill every gap with notes.
>
> Pärt corrected him. "The silence must be longer. This music is about the silence. The sounds are there to surround the silence."
>
> The conductor was baffled, asking, "Exactly how many beats? What do you do during the silence?"
>
> Pärt's response: "You don't do anything. You wait. God does it."[10]

Perhaps the way forward is to tune into the movement of the Spirit, the symphony of the Trinity, and notice what we are being beckoned into. As we are responsive to such movements, we partner with God who is the One Who Does It.

It is a countercultural stance that allows us to converse with our God, who speaks using the many languages of silence. A stance that listens to the silences, and encourages us to learn these nuanced languages, and begin to speak even with the same accent. Waiting and journeying, being still and still moving, silence and speech are all paradoxes. So as we travel we wait, we journey with stillness and attentiveness, learning to speak with silence. And as we wait and learn slowly, God's inexhaustible love comes to us through all silences—whether we know the language well or not—as gift.

The back of the original Rosetta Stone is rough, unpolished and unfinished, and it also has a missing section, sheared off the top at some point in its history. This part of its story is also missing, as yet unknown, untold. So too the sculpting of the Rosetta Stone of the soul and of silence holds an unfinished element, a roughness, a mystery, and there will always be something unknown in the voices of the Divine. The anonymous fourteenth-century author of *The Cloud of Unknowing* writes of such mystery: "the most godlike

---

10. Bouteneff, *Arvo Pärt: Out of Silence*, Kindle location 19–20.

knowledge of God is that which is known by unknowing."[11] The paradox of God coming to us as Word, while one of the central languages of God is silence, means we will always be juggling between speech and silence, yet they are always found one within the other. And just as the Rosetta Stone as we know it is incomplete, with part of it missing from the top, so too this journey into the languages of silence and the soul is not complete, but perhaps it forms a beginning, a taster for what could come next.

The missing part of the Rosetta Stone broke off along an intrusion of pink granite whose crystals can give a tiny gleam in the light. That which intrudes upon our lives, which often results in brokenness, wounds, tears, and pain, is where the balm of the Divine—the tiny pink crystals of light—can meet us. Perhaps many fault lines encountered in the journey may gleam with the One who is Light. And the Rosetta Stone is associated with the town of Thmuis in Egypt, renowned for its perfumed oils and herbs. May the aroma of Christ permeate this journey as we unlock the languages of silence in the spirit of the Rosetta Stone of the soul.

---

11. Wolters, *Cloud of Unknowing*, 137.

2

The Eloquence of Shadows

To make light is to make shadow; one cannot exist without the other. To own one's own shadow is to reach a holy place—an inner center—not attainable in any other way. To fail this is to fail one's own sainthood and to miss the purpose of life.[1]

One companion we have at all times is our shadow. This is the place where we vigorously stuff all those things about ourselves that we don't want to face. We so often try to live in the pretence that none of these characteristics are a part of us, and yet there, trailing behind us—and sometimes in front of us—is our shadow: the shifting shape that reminds us that we are not alone. It is embarrassing, shame-making, and something that we long wasn't with us. We can never disown our shadow, so the discipline of choosing to face and accept parts of our shadow as they are revealed to us is wholesome and holy work. If we can move towards respecting and listening to our shadow, we can glean its wisdom for us. Indeed, as we do this, the Jungian analyst and author Robert Johnson points out, we can then embrace more fully and freely our sainthood, which has been there all along.

1. Johnson, *Owning Your Own Shadow*, 17.

Arriving at the little wooden yurt hidden among the trees, hearing a few cows bellowing in the distance, and sensing the city's demands a long way behind me, this calm place was welcoming me—the whole of me—into its light and shadow.

ENTERING SILENCE

Adjusting

The smell of wood woke me. I gazed around at the many-sided yurt enfolding me with its warm pine-soaked presence. The beams above my head formed what looked like the spokes of a giant wheel holding the thatched roof above. I wondered what kind of ride the day was going to be.

Through the half-open window, I could see the sunlight shafting through the trees and feel the breeze on my face. It was just on sunrise, and the coolness reminded me it wasn't quite summer yet. It was that in-between season, when the air is crisp, and the smell of the dew on the leaves seems to be drawn out by the slow warming of morning.

I lay still, listening to the silence.

I was sure I could hear tiny clicks of movement in the thatching above my head. Some little bugs maybe, waking up slowly and beginning their day of exploration and foraging. . . . I hoped I wouldn't be part of their explorations. I am afraid of spiders, as well as snakes for that matter. So what was I doing then, in the middle of the bush in a little timber hermitage on my own?

As I scrambled up and began to get dressed, I reminded myself that I had come on this retreat as part of my regular discipline of spending time in silence with God, without all the pressure and distractions of everyday demands. I had left my diary at home specifically so I could leave behind my diarized life, and enter into a spaciousness where I could encounter myself and God again.

Grabbing an apple, I wandered out into the unknown day. The ground was still damp from the night and I listened to my footfall sounding felted and soft as I padded down the track toward the river. I shivered. Maybe it was the air, maybe it was the sense that I wasn't the only life-form in this bush. This land had been carefully farmed for years by the monks who dwelt here. I could see the chapel in the distance, on the edge of the property. On previous visits, when I had ventured into the chapel, the walls seemed to hold the deep history of prayers, like woven drapes hanging as warm tapestries of connection. And this morning here in the fields, years of prayerful work seemed to have left the breath of God lingering in the air. I yearned to follow the scent of God.

The river was just a half-hour walk away, and once there the path would lead me through the tea tree forest, down the steep sandy track to the base of the gully, across the river, and up the sandstone escarpment. I could see my breath in the cold air. Breath. The stuff of life.

Clambering over the fence using a stile that reminded me of English walking tracks, I left the retreat acreage behind me and entered the national park. The bush became dense and dark, and the tea trees formed high-arching borders on either side of the path. I pulled absentmindedly at a sprig of tea tree leaves as I passed by and held them to my nose—such a strong smell of tea tree oil, lemon-tangy and fresh. It seemed to clear my head, and I became aware of the old familiar pain in my ankle. A constant companion of mine, and here it was again. It seemed to speak to me through the whispering rhythmic sound of uneven walking, foot . . . *fall*, foot . . . *fall*, foot . . . *fall*.

It was a series of falls in sport that had damaged my ankle when I was at university. I used to run everywhere, enjoyed long-distance running and as many sports events as possible. Two ankle reconstructions later, I am now beginning to feel the mortality of my own body, much to my disgust.

I used to see myself as an irrepressibly unstoppable person, active, lithe, and energetic. I understood that I was in control of my body and to-gether we would go far. Yet who was I now, this limping person who could no longer run at all? Who was this aging person sniffing tea tree oil and walking alone through the bush?

I pondered the tea trees—so gnarled and scrappy, but forming beauti-ful arches over the path. I stopped, and my footfall companion halted its unwelcome tune. I stood in the silence, listening to the morning waking up. Sunlight shafted softly here and there into the leafy tunnel. I was drawn to one single, long, wave-shaped leaf at eye level, and I watched as, very slowly, the stream of sun moved millimeter by millimeter and began touching lightly just the tip of the leaf, then almost caressing in its gentle movement, stroking along its length to the leaf base. My breath had slowed, my heart-beat and even my watching slowed to the pace of the moving sunlight. Time itself felt slow. Then, there seemed the slightest tweak of the leaf tip, giving the tiniest crackle as if it was relaxing in response to the sun's warmth. I felt myself relaxing as the same shaft of sun picked me out in minute motion to touch me on the arm. I quietly slid my hand out of my pocket as if any quick movement would frighten away this shy and delicate beam of light. I held my hand out to let the light fall into the center of my palm.

I was holding the sunlight.

I could see a soft shadow form across my palm as one of my fingers held back a sliver of the sun. My whole body was still, focused, expectant. Each leaf was attentive to the miniscule movements of airborne particles like notes dancing in staves of sun: numinous musical notations. Not even a flutter of breeze. Stillness. Silence and stillness. Yet so full of an exuberant richness.

The sun moved on from my hand, and I became aware of the aromatic smell of the tea trees surrounding me. The sun's warmth was opening the pores of the leaves and the essence was like incense filling the tunnel's sanctuary with its fragrant presence. It was as if the leaves were applauding a concert, responding to the symphonic sunlight with their own morning offering. I breathed it in deeply. Wasn't tea tree oil used as a healing balm? I remembered my mother singing its praises for healing burns, treating infections and bites, and even for household cleaning. I breathed it in again. Is this one of the scents of God? Would it heal my own sense of lost self—the one that used to run and jump and leap through life? Could it be potent enough to help me negotiate a new self, one that was content to walk with a dignified limp? Not only content, but if silence and stillness can somehow be filled with exuberance and richness, could a slower self be filled with the grace and depth of an adagio? Leaping allegros have their place, but without the more reflective ease of the slow musical movements, it would be easy to skid across the top of life and miss plumbing the tonal maple depths of a cello playing Tomaso Albinoni's *Adagio*, or the glowing resin of a walnutty piano piece by Rachmaninov.

The slow symphonic notes had gently lifted my spirit; a sense of God's Spirit and my spirit concurring. Maybe there was some truth in the thought that aging has a future, that the leaping of youth is not all it is cracked up to be. The silence seemed to have become a presence, a healing Presence with a tea tree liturgy of peace. The disturbance within me was far from quiet, but this silence around me seemed to be tending to me like a drawing ointment on an open wound.

Silence as Shadow

I folded a twig of tea tree into my pocket, crushing it deliberately as I put it in, smelling again the wonderful oil. And maybe, just maybe, the tea tree incense was working its healing on my soul. I took one last deep breath, and thanked the treed sanctuary, and ventured on to the sunlit track leading down to the bottom of the gully where the river ran.

The ground was steep, and the track rubbled with loose rocks and tree roots. A recipe for ankle twists. I took it slowly, reminding myself that slow is good, adagios are rich, so I can take my time and respect my natural pace. Halfway down a large rock jutted out over the gully below with a view of the river. I scrambled across the rock and perched on the ledge. Precarious. Precipitous. I needed to notice the way I thought about my past self and my future self. I could easily fall headlong into a dark valley if I didn't take care.

Something made me turn, and I saw my own sitting shadow stretching out behind me. A shadow of my past. I contemplated my shadow—just an outline, made by my body blocking the sun. I swivelled around further and sat facing my shadow, turning my back on the precipice. I guess I hadn't realized just how much the limits set by my ankle really had bothered me. More than bothered, if I was honest, it had goaded me; more than goaded, I felt it had decimated me. I needed to face it head-on.

"I really don't like you. In fact, I am so angry with you I could cry!"

"Tough!" My shadow seemed to speak out of the rock, hard and gritty, with a no-nonsense voice. "I am here to stay!"

"Well, that's rude . . . and true," I thought. I reached for a nearby branch and started tracing out my shadow across the sandstone. My shadow kept moving, it seemed to be mimicking me, mocking me. I started to get angrier.

"I am angry! I am angry you are here. I am so sad I have lost any capacity to run any more. I am just so deeply bereft." It was this last word, "bereft," that undid me.

Inside my body a dam wall gave way, and I just wept. The freedom to cry out loud to all the leaves and the unseen bugs and animals, and not to feel judged by them as they held witness to my sorrow was freeing and releasing. Slowly, as my sobs abated, I noticed how quickly the warm rock was evaporating my tears. I became fascinated. It was as if the sun and the rock together received my tears, changing them from water to vapor, and letting them become airborne. I took another look at my shadow as it reflected the outline of me so accurately and without embellishment.

I continued gazing at this shadow, and I could see it mirroring my inner darkness, my inner shadow. My heart was thumping in my chest, and my breathing was labored. All this fear inside—of aging, loss, change. There was nowhere to run—quite literally—anymore. So I decided to risk continuing a conversation with this rocky, shadowy personality.

"You really are always going to be with me, aren't you?" I stood up, and my shadow stood with me. I turned, and looked over my shoulder as if to check—yes, my shadow turned too.

"But how do I make friends with you? I know this sounds silly—you are just a shadow. But you are always there, reminding me of what I do not want to see."

"So that's it then. Just a shadow, am I? Come up with something more creative, a shadow of what?"

"A shadow of my former self," I replied, thinking it was a clever response, but not sure quite what I meant by it.

"Friends have names. I dare you to name me."

I pondered. It had to be something to do with my past self. What about "Passé"—a conflation of "past self"! I began to roll the name around in my mouth. "Passé" . . . well, how delightful to refer to this past self as outmoded, out-of-date, even quaint. That was a new take. I could do this.

"What about 'Passé'?" I said triumphantly.

The response was quick. "Now that's got a ring about it. That'll do."

"Time to move on," I said, referring to both the walk and the issue. I was aware of my discomfort with this discussion.

"Wait for me," said my new friend. And we started off down the track again, not hand in hand, but touching foot to foot.

I slid the last few metres to the gully floor, and edged my way along the rocks banking the river. The sun was streaming down by now, and I bent to drink from the clear water. I started making my way towards the place where the rocks were high enough to allow me to cross the river to the other side. It wasn't a wide river, maybe a few metres only and not very deep, but I didn't want to be walking with wet shoes.

After some while, I saw the crossing up ahead. I scrambled over and picked my way gingerly across the river, rock to rock, taking care to listen to my ankle and respond to what it needed to keep the rest of me upright and confident. This was the beginning of my new self, after all, a dignified adagio and I needed to give it the respectful hearing it deserved.

The sound of the river chasing its way between the rocks pummelled my ears after the previous silence of the bush, and I found I was anxious to move away from the torrent of noise. Grasping clumps of grass and a branch here and there, I began to make my way slowly up the other side.

The other side—it felt like I had indeed crossed an interior Rubicon, and was beginning a fresh venture. This felt new, with a strength and resolve that I hadn't felt before. Beginning to embrace my new self, and with the candid companionship of Passé, I was slowly moving forward. I paused and took a few deep breaths, noticing that now the smells were no longer of tea tree but of damp earth, a dark humus-smell, as if all the old rotting fallen leaves, the stuff of the past, were now being made into rich fecund soil ready for new life. The smell of a deep earthy silent Presence rose from the ground, and with it, strength from having encountered my shadow face-to-face.

Epiphanies of the Moment

Beginning the climb again, I noticed the way my arms and hands stretched forwards to find the next handhold, tree trunk, or rock to pull myself up with. A bit like reaching forward for who I was becoming. I realized that it was all very well to make friends with (and even joke about) my past self, but what about making friends with who I am yet to be? Or was I too anxiously clambering and grasping for footholds in a future that hadn't yet emerged? The questions kept tumbling: Who did I want to be? Who was I being invited to be? And how would I greet my future self? "This limping self," I muttered under my breath in disgust. It's hard to leave behind old habits.

I had reached a section where the track traversed two huge sloping boulders that met each other at their base, making the path into the form of a sharp V-shape through the tight crevice; and then further up I could see the path continuing. I moved forward, a bit uncertain how I could navigate this.

I put my good foot forward. The right way to start, I thought. I wedged that foot in, and then found some handholds, and lifted up my other foot and placed it just ahead. All good. Until I tried to lift my good foot out of the crevice to take the next step. It was firmly wedged, too firmly wedged. I couldn't move it. In fact, I couldn't really move. I leaned my shoulder against the rock face, and took a few deep breaths. It would be fine—I just had to take it easy and go slow. Wasn't that what I had learnt from the tea tree tunnel? To slow down, be still, and be stilled by the silence? I looked down and again tried to move my good foot. A slight something, but was it taking me deeper in? Maybe I could wriggle my foot out of my shoe and get out of it that way. But I had done too good a job securing my walking shoes so there would be little slippage and no chance of twisted ankles. The crevice was so narrow, I could hardly bend. To think of undoing my laces on my back shoe behind me would involve contortions I certainly couldn't perform.

When in doubt, I told myself, breathe.

"So, what is this about?" I asked my new friend. "What's going on?"

"Well, you are asking for wisdom from your 'Passé' past. Are you sure you want that kind of wisdom?"

"I have made friends with you, right? So that means you have my best interest at heart, I assume. I think wisdom is wisdom, regardless of what era it comes from. I'm ready." Was I sounding more convinced than I really felt? What option did I have?

"Well, look at your feet."

"I have been! What do you think I've been doing?" I was frustrated, and wondering about my own wisdom at this point.

"Don't you speak to others a lot about being in the moment, about being in the present? Your current dilemma is a rather awkward metaphor for you, don't you think?"

I looked down at my feet. They were at odd angles and securely wedged, particularly the back one. I couldn't move. I began to see what my shadow was pointing out, but I still resisted. What was I doing here in this great discomfort with an enigmatic shadow talking in riddles to me?

"Look down," Passé said calmly. "What do you see?"

"I see two feet stuck in a crevice."

"And where have you been spending so much of your time?" Passé was speaking with some sensitivity now, perhaps at last aware that I was beginning to feel a bit fragile.

Frustrated, fearful, and close to tears I replied, "Talking to you, I think!"

"Exactly right," Passé chimed. "You have either been in the past or grasping hurriedly for the future. This is your opportunity to be fully where you are and let it teach you. All the answers you need in order to take the next step will be here, in this present moment at your feet."

It all slowly began to dawn on me. Having begun to accept my past self, I was now hurriedly groping for the future. But what about now—this very now? Where was I right now and more importantly who was I right now? How does one leave the past and not stride immediately into the future, but rather slide down into the wisdom and wealth of the present? Here my feet were holding me to this time and this space. I couldn't go back. I couldn't go forward.

"OK. I get it." I was beginning to let go of my annoyance. "I am trapped in the now. I need to make friends with who I am right now—a pilgrim on the journey toward being a contented adagio limper. Actually, change that to a nomad. For nomads the journey is the destination. Does that pass the test?"

Passé replied thoughtfully, "Nomad. That makes a lot of sense. I like that! Nomads are always on the move; and so perhaps it's time you started moving. Start with where you are now. Listen to what the present is teaching you."

I thought it was easier said than done. But I had a strange feeling, something like the absence of worry or fear. I somehow knew I just had to take the time to wriggle my stronger foot in the right way and it would eventually come free. I shifted my weight to my bad foot, leaving my wedged foot free from any downward pressure. There was no place for hurry in this. I began to slowly twitch my toes and then wriggle my foot within the shoe, just tiny movements. The sandstone was soft, and tiny crystal fragments around my shoe came away, but nothing at all large enough for me to become free. As I looked at my foot, I realized that here I was, at last attentive to this one place in space and time, the "now" as my shadow had named it.

I kept wriggling my foot. I shifted the angle of my body and leaned towards the other side of the crevice, my ankle tipped into an unnatural shape, and for a moment I feared I had made things worse. But just then, release! The laces had all become just fractionally looser, my foot minutely freer to move and change shape, and my shoe came free. I breathed a huge sigh of relief. Leaning my back against one side of the crevice, I carefully lifted up both feet and placed them flat against the opposite side of the crevice, and straddled the space over the wedge—the wedge of now.

I was freely straddling the now, but no longer trapped in it. I had been caught by the foot, tripped up, and brought to the point where I could do nothing other than be fully attentive to the present. This was a lesson I wanted to remember, to be fully attentive to the present, and let it reveal the minutiae of clues toward ways of moving onwards.

"Whew! I'm exhausted after that," I sighed out loud as I leaned my head back against the rock and looked up at the blue sky with all its vast clarity. I cast a glance at Passé, mostly hidden behind my back, perhaps even guarding my back. "Thanks for keeping me company and giving me what I needed to pay attention. I think adagio is definitely my new rhythm for my present self—slower, more attentive, reflective, able to listen to the now in order to take the next step."

"Sounds good to me," Passé reflected back. "Are you thinking of a cello or a piano for your adagio?"

I pondered the possibilities for a bit, and then recalled the komuz, a hauntingly beautiful three-stringed instrument of the Kyrgyz nomads I had read about and watched on YouTube. Its rhythm seemed always to be that of a deep resonant slowness that drew me down into my own rich depths. Three strings and no frets. The three strings seemed to offer a Trinity of companionship in making the music, and the lack of fretting—well that was a play on words that made a lot of sense to me. Komuz. Perhaps that was it.

"I think it is a komuz, and maybe that is my new name—an adagio instrument for nomads." I felt at last I had arrived at the present. A good place to be, with a name that gave music I could travel to. I was grateful for the journey with my shadow. I was able now to smile at my shadow! Passé seemed to smile back at me. I waved—and it waved back. Ah, the eloquence of shadows.

Deeper into the Tree Rings of Silence

The next day I headed out in the afternoon, this time through the forest to a clearing at the top of the hill. I walked slowly into the silence awaiting me: internal silence and external silence. A deep sense of contentment pervaded my whole being, and I found a tree to sit up against as I settled in to absorb the wonder of this presence.

The silence seemed to sing. It was a silence that had an intensely personal presence to it—that sense you get when there is a deeply loved one in the room, with whom there is a great deal of harmony and resonance. It reminded me of a time when I was staying with a friend in the Blue Mountains.

One windless day, she took her violin and together we went deep into the forest below our cabin. We found a very small clearing in the midst of a stand of giant eucalyptus trees, where the bark was scattered in thick curling layers on the ground and the ancient tree ferns in the gully below opened out with ecstatic green fronds unfurling towards the sky. Here we stopped, and in this tree-filled concert hall, she played her violin. It was as if the wood of her violin was resonating and echoing with the wood of the trees. Both woods knew what it was like to embody the voices and sounds of the forest—the thousands of birdsongs that had left notes hanging onto the branches like Christmas baubles; the seasons of rains and heat forming the inner rings in patterns of growth; the sounds of breezes and winds that filled the wood with infinite vibrations and tones; and the colors of dark and light woven into the gnarled trunks.

As I listened to the trees around me now, it was as if the Trinitarian God was playing a slow adagio on the komuz and I was hearing it deeply through the earth, feeling it thudding in my sternum. "O Trinity, you are music, you are life," prayed Hildegard of Bingen, the twelfth-century abbess and musician.[2] For Hildegard, "all of creation is a song of praise to God."[3] I had come through noisiness from my questions and fears that morning and had now emerged into the deep silence of the clearing, bathing in the stillness of simply being with this Trinitarian God. I was still. So still. Slowly the singing silence faded into a warm deep presence that I simply yielded to seamlessly, effortlessly. All the echoes from the forest of my thoughts had long given way. The slow adagio had stopped its playing, and the rich, full earthiness of God breathed new life into me. The scent of God. I breathed

---

2. Uhlein, *Meditations with Hildegard of Bingen*, 37.
3. Uhlein, *Meditations with Hildegard of Bingen*, 40.

God in, and God breathed me in. This breathing was like a conversation that was beyond words, a conversation with silence.

REFLECTION

Shadows and Metaphors to Travel By

I noticed on the retreat how I was grappling and arguing with my shadow, wrestling with God-in-my-shadow, perhaps not dissimilar to Jacob's wrestling through the night with God at Jabbok (Gen 32:22–31). Jacob wasn't wrestling simply with a person, but slowly realized he was striving with God's very self. And his struggle was reflected his inner battle with his false self and his own shadow. So too, I was not tussling simply with my physical shadow, but with God and my own inner dark shadow. God gave Jacob the new name of Israel, meaning one who struggled with God and prevailed. And I conjured up a new name for my shadow. Such new names help us move forward into our newly becoming selves. Jacob emerges with a limp, and I wonder what this limp meant for him over the coming years? How did he manage his decreased mobility and speed? And what memories and lessons did his damaged hip continue to teach him?

But I also had a sense of the wrestling with my shadow turning more into a dance. The concept of "adagio" had come to me during the experience, but as I have reflected and read further, I notice that adagios also refer to the part of a dance that is called "pas de deux." This is where a dancer and her partner perform a dancing discourse together with a succession of lyrical, fluid, slow movements. We can sometimes reach a point with part of our shadow selves where we move into a pas de deux: a dance choreographed by the Spirit, with surprising discourse and intimate moments of vulnerability and self-disclosure.

"To honor and accept one's own shadow is a profound spiritual discipline. It is whole-making and thus holy and the most important experience of a lifetime."[4] Our shadows are those parts of the self that none of us wants to see, so we try to hide them from ourselves and everyone else. To confront our shadow is to find our own light. Richard Rohr points out that Jesus and the prophets challenged Israel's corporate and individual shadows. "It is in the struggle with our shadow self, with failure, or with wounding that we break into higher levels of consciousness. People who learn to expose, name, and still thrive inside the contradictions are people I would call prophets."[5]

4 Johnson, *Owning Your Own Shadow*, Introduction, para. 5.

5. Rohr, "Struggling with Shadow," 1.

Perhaps the shadow is one of the greatest teachers regarding how to come to the light, to engage with our shadow when it is revealed, and use our imaginations to dialogue with it. This does not mean we are wasting our time with useless make-believe. On the contrary, it enables that which is ungraspable by rational means to be apprehended and described, then transformed. For example, imaginary numbers are a necessity used to describe and solve electrical, mechanical, engineering, and architectural problems that would otherwise not be possible. So too, imaginary dialogues used in prayer can enable us to hear ourselves more clearly and hear God more loudly in the service of becoming more whole, becoming transfigured.

Werner G. Jeanrond, an Oslo-based theologian particularly interested in transcendence and transformation, suggests silence opens us to face our "inner self—its complex web of voices, dreams, desires, fears and bleeding wounds of the soul. It may at first feel threatening when allowing a confrontation with all the expressions of my inner self which sound strange, shockingly other and at times appear in direct opposition to my ordinary self-perception."[6] He asks how we can love the inner chaos and darkness in our emerging selves. To find the answer he leans into the wisdom of spiritual writers such as Teresa of Avila, Thomas Merton, Ignatius, and others who give guidance on how to embrace the companionship of God in our inner selves.

Barry MacDonald, in his preface to John Chryssavgis's work on the desert fathers and mothers, reminds us that "the demons fight hardest when God is near; the darkness of the shadow is in direct proportion to the brilliance of the light."[7] It is important to note that because the shadow is made up of those aspects of ourselves that we haven't integrated and often are running from, the shadow also holds not only our darkness, but also the gold of our best selves that we have rejected. This will be discussed in the section "For Further Engagement" later in this chapter.

Silence as Healer

Silence has a way of allowing things we have been avoiding to rise up to the surface, to be addressed by the One who is Healer. Sometimes distractions are simply that—distractions from prayer and a way to escape from prayer and from coming face to face with Mystery. But this time, what was being drawn up from within me wasn't a distraction to be ignored. Rather, God was using the silence to allow all the issues surrounding my ankle to rise up.

6. Jeanrond, "Love and Silence," 20.

7. Chryssavgis, *In the Heart of the Desert*, Preface, para. 5.

Slowly it became clear that this was God's agenda. Martin Laird, an Augustinian friar and academic specializing in early Christian studies, captures this when he says, "Silence is sometimes like a poultice placed over a sore to draw out infection as part of the healing process."[8] God was using this spacious time of silence to place a poultice on an area of deep pain, drawing up to the surface all the poison of fear, anger, and sense of loss I had pushed down for some years.

Even as I reflect now, I notice a new awareness rising: that of disappointment—a word that didn't come to me on that particular day at all, but as the poultice continues to work, I feel the heavy traces of disappointment. And more than that, it now occurs to me there is also a sense of dispossession. Disappointment and dispossession seem to be coursing through me like toxic, slow runnels. One step forward, two steps back. Healing seems so slow. As I sit with these words, I am suddenly aware of the word "ointment" in the midst of "disapp-*ointment*," forming part of one of these word-runnels. It feels trite to see this wordplay. And yet perhaps here again is the poultice at work. As I turn this to prayer, what seem to be heavy and backward steps of such strong streams of disappointment and dispossession, may—if I am humble enough—contain the very healing ointment I need. The toxins are being flushed to the surface. Staying with what is being held up to us for attention can require commitment and discipline to take the time for further silent reflection and avoid escaping into activity.

Laird encourages us to continue being with what has arisen for us. And sometimes that may be a woundedness that has come to meet us. He says, "All wounds flower. We only need to investigate, by looking straight into the wound. Only interior silence can look deeply into a wound. What silence finds is also silent."[9] The present moment is rich with God's own restorative and healing presence and, if we miss this, we can be left the poorer for it, bereft, and somehow knowing we have turned from facing truth. We can take solace and courage when we know that our wounds are not empty and gaping, but rather, as we gaze on our pain, we are gazing upon the One who took all our woundedness into God's own body.

Some forms of struggle and woundedness can plunge us into the death-like tombs we are carrying within; dark places and inner demons that we understandably do all we can to avoid. The Jesuit mystic Anthony de Mello (1931–87) reminds us that even though it means we need to go through an interior land of death, it may be the required path to reach Love, who

8. Laird, *Sunlit Absence*, 49.
9. Laird, *Ocean of Light*, 217.

births us into resurrection after resurrection.[10] It is worth remembering that in the darkness of the tombs of both Jesus and Lazarus, in the aloneness, tenebrosity, and heaviness of those dreaded places, new life and resurrection happened. And the person, known as the demoniac who dwelt among the tombs outside Gerasene, was released as a result of his encounter with Jesus (Mark 5:1–17). So our "tombs" too, are places where it is possible to experience resurrection and release.

When we invite the God of infinite love to be with us to surround and guide us, we can dare to be vulnerable. We can bathe in this Love as if we were to immerse ourselves into a deep still lake, naked, and having nothing to protect, nothing to pretend, and nothing to defend about ourselves. Such can be the cleansing and healing balm of God, whom we can name as Loving Silence. Mysterious, sometimes painful, yet always healing, silence surely is a "medicine we need."[11]

This Clear and Shining Moment

When I think of the role nature has in enabling me to slow down and to enter into silence, the word "Sherpa" comes to my mind. Nature so often is my gentle Sherpa, skilled and knowing the territory of silence so well, I am guided into deeper knowledge and awareness of what is right before my eyes—all that is so sensorially rich—yet it is so easy to miss. It was this nature, my Sherpa, that ushered me via the tea tree tunnel into my own heartbeat and the sound of my breathing, and attuned me to the tiny leaf with a curling tip. Such attentiveness to the present moment can then become a doorway through which we enter into the numinous mystery of God's ineffable presence.

"The present moment is our home."[12] I wonder at the number of times when Jesus has probably come knocking on the doors of our homes (Rev 3:20) and yet we simply have chosen not to hear, being preoccupied with internal discussions about the past or multiple concerns about the future. But the present moment is the time and place in which we live, in which the Incarnate One approaches us. We can be so caught up in a conversation around the meal table that we find we have finished the meal and not been aware and present to how it tasted at all. Such preoccupation distracted the two people walking on the road to Emmaus (Luke 24:13–35). They only discovered later on reflection that, in their absorption with fear and painful

---

10. De Mello, *Way to Love*.

11. Bennett, "Endangered Habitat," 67.

12. Laird, *Ocean of Light*, 53.

confusion, they had missed being aware of the very visceral sense that their hearts were "burning within." They had not been able to be attentive to the wisdom of their own bodies, alerting them to a mystery in their midst.

It can be so simple and yet so difficult to live mindfully, even when on a retreat; to be fully present and surrendered to each moment so that we might encounter the Sacred. Within each moment dwells God. "How clear and shining this way is!" declares de Caussade, the eighteenth-century Jesuit. And to avail ourselves of such an encounter, de Caussade encourages us to approach the present moment in such a way that "the soul, light as a feather, fluid as water, innocent as a child, responds to every movement of grace like a floating balloon."[13] Such moment-by-moment surrender to the Spirit who moves mysteriously is an art of sacred living that is worth cultivating.

Anthony Bloom (1914–2003), the Russian Orthodox archbishop, offers very practical exercises for learning to be in the present moment. He suggests we simply sit still in the presence of ourselves and of God. He points out that many will feel bored. He suggests this is the result of being in an unhealthy way "completely empty, we do not act from within ourselves but accept as our life a life which is actually fed in from outside; we are used to things happening which compel us to do other things. How seldom can we live simply by means of the depth and the richness we assume that there is within ourselves."[14] Bloom goes on to point out that our emptiness inevitably affects the way we relate to others and to God, urging us to practice being in the present alone with God.

To live mindfully is also to bring a compassionate and nonjudgmental awareness to what is happening in our thoughts, bodies, and emotions. In this way, we partner with our God, who has infinite compassion and is nonjudgmental. Paul's words counter so much of church dogma, when he says, "do you despise the riches of [God's] kindness and forbearance and patience? Do you not realize that God's kindness is meant to lead you to repentance?" (Rom 2:4). It is in this safe and loving Presence that we can "face whatever comes to us calmly and courageously, knowing we have the flexibility to weather any storm gracefully."[15]

De Caussade exclaims that we so often look for God everywhere except within this very present moment. Mindfulness is an art, honing us to "be responsive to the slightest prompting from these almost imperceptible

---

13. De Caussade, *Abandonment*, 22.

14. Bloom, *Beginning to Pray*, 68.

15. Easwaran, *Conquest of Mind*, 49.

impulses." He continues, "Each moment is a revelation of God."[16] The present moment can be both epiphany and sacrament.

PONDERING YOUR OWN EXPERIENCES

Our experiences are important, no matter how small, trite, or even clichéd they may feel. They are worth valuing as gifts of grace from God. To take time to reflect on these honors our experience and continues to unwrap the treasures of our transfiguration. Below are some suggestions for pondering your own experiences.

- "I had left my diary at home specifically so I could leave behind my diarized life, and enter into a spaciousness where I could encounter myself and God again." What is your diarized life like, and how would you like to change it? What can you put in place to allow it to reflect more accurately your deepest desires for your life? What may be your fears or presuppositions about silence?

- It can be a long journey from wanting to fill our already cluttered lives with good experiences and useful things, to the place of release and surrender so that we may find an interior spaciousness in which to encounter God. Sometimes our hands and our lives are so full, we have no space to receive what the Spirit is offering. You may wish to set aside some time to be silent, and to reflect on your own experiences of journeying through shades of letting go and the way silence has engaged you in different ways. What fills your hands, and what needs to be let go of, in order to receive that ineffable Presence?

- "I continued gazing at this shadow, and I could see it mirroring my inner darkness, my inner shadow." Is there an inner darkness within you that is begging to be addressed? Can you listen to what it wants you to know? You may want to give this darkness or shadow a name, and then invite it into a conversation with yourself and with a member of the Trinity as well. What is said between the three of you? What healing might God be inviting you into?

- Journaling can be a helpful way of recording our experiences in prayer, but for transformation to happen there needs to be reflection on our times spent in silence. Choose a significant experience you have had of silence, perhaps from your journal or lodged within your memory. Take the time to reenter that experience, and allow yourself to notice

16. De Caussade, *Abandonment*, 16.

how that particular silence may have had some colors, textures, sounds, aromas, or tastes for you. Silence may also have touched into senses we have that are not physical—such as a sense of presence, the Holy, or "otherness"; of being apprehended, beckoned, observed, loved, enjoyed, affirmed. Perhaps God came to you embodying silence as a partner in a dance, as a Wise Guide, or conversing with you through a part of yourself or through a metaphor or something in nature. Allow what may have been up until now simply notes written as sheet music to be brought to life again by the Spirit and let it sing its own transformative song within you. You may wish to journal this second reflection, which will help you treasure it and remember it.

FOR FURTHER ENGAGEMENT

Distractions May Also Be Stepping-Stones

Is a "distraction" simply that—a deviation from the real work of contemplative prayer, merely inner noise and fleeting or persistent intrusions that are better left alone? Or are these distractions forming stepping-stones toward that deeper contemplative silence in which all thoughts can then evaporate in the presence of Presence? Discernment helps us to know when distractions are pulling us away from intimacy with God, or when the Spirit is using the opportunity of our being in silence to allow wounds or issues to be brought to the surface for us to address together with the one who is the Healer. Laird takes the view that "distractions are a given in the practice of contemplation; our practice cannot deepen without them. What changes over the course of time is our relationship with them. Gradually we see that distractions contain within themselves the silence we seek; therefore, we do not have to be rid of them in order for our practice of contemplation to open up."[17] He also offers a caution:

> The seduction is to think we can use our practice of contemplation as a way to avoid facing our woundedness: if we can just go deeply enough into contemplation, we won't struggle any longer. It is common enough to find people taking a cosmetic view of contemplation . . . and then discover that they still have the same old warts and struggles they hoped contemplation

17. Laird, *Sunlit Absence*, 5.

would remove or hide. They think that somewhere they must have gone wrong.[18]

When we are able to take ourselves on a silent retreat that is longer that a couple of days, there may be times when our woundedness needs to be faced in order for us to grow in deeper intimacy with the One whom we love. And we can do this in the presence of God, who is deeply loving and nonjudgmental, who formed us in our mother's womb and knows us better than we know ourselves. In which case, to resist conversing with this woundedness would be to resist the gentle promptings of the Spirit. Our pain and struggle may well be the dark tunnel through which the pathway leads into a new and deeper intimacy that will unfold over the beckoning silence that awaits us.

There are other times when distractions come like pestering flies that don't want to leave us alone. In these times, we could do well to take advice from the author of *The Cloud of Unknowing* to look over the shoulders of the distractions as it were, searching for something else—and that something is God, enclosed in the cloud of unknowing.[19] Discerning the difference may take some time, and here it is helpful to have a wise guide to confer with, such as a spiritual director, or one who offers spiritual accompaniment.

Shadow Work: Light out of Darkness

As we traverse the landscapes of silence, we may often experience periods of deep shadow, or even a kind of existential blackout. Finding our way through these precipitous landscapes can take a long time. Such experiences of spiritual darkness can turn our worlds upside down, disorienting us, and opening up a yawning trapdoor that appears bottomless and threatens annihilation.

There are times when a darkness we are experiencing takes the form of a shadow, embodying parts of ourselves that we disdain and have unconsciously disowned. Acknowledging our shadow simply means we are admitting we have many parts to us, much of which we keep to ourselves, and some of which we keep *from* ourselves. When we continue to refuse to face our darkness, we are stuffing these shadows into an old carpet bag that will eventually burst its seams in the most unhelpful place and in very destructive ways. One of those damaging consequences is when we project what we disdain in ourselves onto others, thus creating a scapegoat[20] as a

---

18. Laird, *Into the Silent Land*, 118.
19. Wolters, *Cloud of Unknowing*.
20. See work done on the concept of scapegoating by René Girard and James Alison.

way of sending our darkness into the desert, and cheating ourselves into thinking none of that darkness belongs with us. We have seen the destructive results of this in many churches and society where people have insisted on celebrating and worshipping only our light, and have refused a place in their theology for the welcoming and processing of our darkness, and the subsequent gifts that can come forth.

When such a dark shadow rises up and confronts us, however unwelcome such an appearance may be, it always comes to us for the purposes of healing, wholeness, and integration. Such a confrontation can fill us with fear and apprehension; we fear we have taken a wrong turn and can feel completely lost and at sea. Connie Zweig, well-known for her writing on shadow work, offers a word of hope when she says, "when we enter the night sea journey, as Jung called it, we are not off the path; we are on it. In fact, we may be spot on it, right where we belong."[21] If we can stay with this "right place," and address our shadow and allow it to address us, we can begin to receive the healing, the light out of darkness that will slowly dawn from it.

It is important to mention also that there is gold that lies within our shadows: those honorable and wondrous parts of ourselves that we resist acknowledging and owning. And sometimes this golden part of our shadow can be extremely difficult for us to accept. Robert Johnson has an apt way of putting it: "It is more disrupting to find that you have a profound nobility of character than to find out you are a bum. . . . Ignoring the gold can be as damaging as ignoring the dark side of the psyche."[22] Our contribution to the healing of ourselves and to the way we live in our societies is to grow in the courage to face our shadow selves.

The Long Path to the Inner Silence of Contemplative Prayer

The pathway into contemplative depths can defy description. But some have used transformative stages as a way to express the path, which have variously been expressed as including kataphatic (images and word-based prayer) and apophatic (imageless, wordless prayer); knowing and unknowing (a dark, preconceptual knowing); John of the Cross's dark nights of the senses and of the spirit; purgative, illuminative, and unitive ways;[23] *via positiva, via*

---

21. Zweig, *Meeting the Shadow of Spirituality*, Kindle location 271.

22. Johnson, *Owning Your Own Shadow*, 8.

23. Johnston, *Mystical Theology*.

negativa, via creativa, via transformitiva;[24] and for some it may include the stage of *via feminina.*[25]

Because the journey is lifelong, these may be seen as stations that the mystic travels through in prayer, and does so at repeatedly deeper and deeper levels as purification slowly molds the mystic character. It is not a "going back" to a previous stage, but rather "going on" to a new stage. It is a movement forward because each person—under the shaping hand of the Infinite One, who is the "pioneer and perfecter of our faith" (Heb 12:2)—is "being transformed . . . from one degree of glory to another" (2 Cor 3:18). So we come anew to revisit a station or stage, yet each time it may be on a deeper level. Teasdale suggests seven levels of transformation as part of this theosis in the mystical formation of character.[26] Metaphors, paradoxes, and koans[27] provide stepping-stones to what is beyond explanation, enticing a response from us, by which, through the flame of unknowing, a sublime wisdom is wrought, and where infused and acquired giftings may meet.

Use of the Imagination: When Silence Apprehends Us

Guite claims that "our imagination is part of the Imago Dei in us."[28] There is much in the world and about ourselves that is able to be understood through our rational faculty. However, there are some things that only the imagination can articulate and name. The rational, as Guite states, is able to help us comprehend, while the imagination enables us to apprehend.

Jesus assumed his hearers would use their imaginations: when he told a parable, he relied on his audience to fill in the details. And we know from writers such as Henri Nouwen[29] that the more we let ourselves get right inside these stories of Jesus in great detail, the more we discover about God and ourselves, and the more transformative is the experience. Imagination draws in the whole person, so that engagement at the levels of heart and body can occur. Scripture is a place of encounter with the living God, and our imaginations and our reasoning are the two feet with which we walk

24. Fox, *Spirituality Named Compassion.*

25. Lanzetta, *Radical Wisdom.*

26. Teasdale, *Mystic Heart.*

27. A koan is a riddle that invites us to engage our intuition rather than simply relying on logical reasoning, and is used to demonstrate that spiritual and personal growth is a mystery, drawing on rational, intuitive, and imaginative engagement.

28. Guite, *Faith, Hope and Poetry*, 12.

29. Nouwen, *Return of the Prodigal Son.*

into this measureless world of the Word. We need both the rational and the imagination, and God's transforming Spirit uses both with us.

So when we are able to spend some days in silence, we can take the time to explore our relationship with this God who is Word, Love, and Silence, and we may find that not only do we apprehend Silence but this Silence also apprehends us. We can surrender ourselves not only to speak with Silence, but Silence may speak with us; we may even wrestle with Silence, and Silence may wrestle with us, just as Jacob and the Messenger wrestled by the river Jabbok. We can be taken by surprise by this God who initiates surprises.

One of the important things to do at the outset of a retreat, or any time of silence and solitude we choose to enter, is to notice what agenda we have come with. We need to do the difficult work of surrendering our agendas and expectations as much as possible in order to allow the God who speaks through all things to be the Guide. It may feel disorienting and vulnerable to do this, to let God be the one in control, yet surely that is what we would want. For what kind of God would it be if we were to wrestle with this God, and win?

3

Eating Honey with God

For it is not knowing much, but realizing and relishing things interiorly, that contents and satisfies the soul.[1]

"Relish" is a luxurious word, not ordinarily associated with deserts. Those who have ventured into the desert long enough to go beyond seeing it as romantic know how desert experiences can be harsh and threatening, taking us to the very edge of our capacity to stay alive. The desert landscape can be seen as a book, which we read and which also reads us. We may find lyrical beauty in its messages, or we may be cut to the quick with its incisive ability to splay us open beneath an unrelenting sun. There may be little comfort, a bit like the books the Jewish Bohemian-born author Franz Kafka advocated, when he suggested we need authors who are "like pick axes" that chip away our small assumptions and cramped life-paradigms.[2] It may only be years later that we are courageous enough to ruminate on such an experience, and be able to reflect without flinching. We may even find something we learned that so rings of deep truth that it tastes sweeter than honey, though perhaps wild honey, with a sharp edge.

1. Ignatius of Loyola, *Spiritual Exercises*, xxv.
2. Kafka, *Letters to Friends*, 16.

Outback Australia has become one of those places of relishing for me. I had arranged to meet Old Madge near the large stand of mulga trees just off the Callum Track road. I parked my car, and made my way across the dry red dirt and small scrub bush. I could see her there already. Waiting for me.

RELISHING THE DESERT SILENCE

Desert Honey and Images of God

Old Madge carefully held up the small grape-sized golden orb to her ninety-year-old lips. Wizened and beautiful as she was, I couldn't help but think, "This is Grandmother God I am sitting with." She neatly bit the golden orb from the rest of the ant she was holding and, as the liquid amber burst into her mouth, she grinned with the sweetness, and wiped the honey-colored trickle from her chin.

This was a lesson in desert wisdom from Old Madge, as I watched her search instinctively for the honeypot ants' nests and know just how deep to dig for them. These ants live up to four metres underground, she told me. Native to the Australian dry interior areas, the ants sustain themselves through the desert barrenness by setting aside some of their colony called repletes, whose sole purpose is to store nectar in their abdomens, which slowly expand to the size of a large grape, and shine like transparent honey-pots. Unable to move with the weight, they hang like golden baubles from the ceiling inside the ants' nest about a metre from the surface, and are fed by the worker ants a drop at a time. During times of food shortage, when the yellow-flowering mulga or the delicate purple desert fuchsias are too dry to offer nectar, the worker ants then feed from their honeypot companions. Old Madge wanted me to taste this surprising sweet treasure, a true desert delicacy.

I gingerly picked one up by the head and as swiftly as possible bit down on the abdomen rupturing the golden orb that covered my tongue in warm syrupy fullness. Remarkably sweet but with a spicy tang, the taste seemed so much greater than the small drop I had expected. I glanced at Old Madge. Her dark milky eyes were laughing and her round-plum cheeks were amused at this city person encountering the treats of the land.

It had been such a good morning, walking through the mulgas with Madge. Watching her was like observing a guardian of the landscape, like a great eagle, hovering over the surface, seeing everything. It was more than her home that she was walking through, moving so silently in tune with the silence around us. It was as if her interior landscape had melded with the external landscape and all was one. She wasn't *at* home, she *was* home. And being alongside her seemed to enable me also to become attuned to the silence, a bit like the concert master giving the note so that others could tune to the same note. This was a silence tuned to hospitality and welcome, enveloping me like a hearty embrace, strong and joyful. I felt as if all the pores of my being were opening as wide as possible to absorb every drop of this golden-honeyed silence.

We had settled under a large mulga tree; there was no hurry, no time pressure. I don't know how long we sat there together, each absorbed in our own world. After a time, I looked over at Old Madge. I had noticed a kind of centeredness in her; she was earthed yet alight, wholesome and free. Yes, she embodied Grandmother God to me that day.

"God?" she responded, after I had ventured to ask about her God. "God's everywhere—in you, in me, everywhere. Look, you can feel, touch. God's here alright. You just gotta savor, stand still and listen, feel, and know. That's how you know. That's how knowing comes. That's the real peace. Just be still. Savor."

And so we continued to sit in the stillness among the mulgas and the heat and the ants underground. We seemed to blend in with the shimmering heat of this hot desert silence. Stillness in God. This was a Grandmother Silence speaking gently words resonant of the wonder and tranquillity that my grandmother's sunroom had for me as a child: an all-encompassing embrace that says, I know you, your history has roots within me, you belong. Come—let's drink tea together.

Sitting with these tea- and honey-drinking grandmothers, I became aware of something like a doorstop wedge jammed under my stomach. I had for so long bowed under the heaviness of a patriarchal church with its male language and hierarchy and had been deeply wounded many times. One such incident occurred at a very formative time, when as a student at university I was asked by my church minister to lead worship over the Easter weekend. Both he and I were challenged by members in the church, one of whom was shaking with emotion, saying: "You cannot lead worship as a female; you will grieve the Holy Spirit." And the minister conceded. And after completing theological degrees, and applying for a job in a church, I was very clearly being informed that there would not be a job for me, as I was a female.

After all these years, the Spirit was again touching in to my old painful memories that lay scattered like a selection of broken teacups on the floor of my soul, each holding a sense of hollowness and insufficiency. And yet now, Grandmother God was tenderly picking up one or two of these cracked cups and, as we sat in this sunroom, she began pouring in a tea of warm balm and spices. For a moment, I felt I could indeed taste something of that "knowing" Madge spoke of in the honey on my tongue.

Wide Sky Holiness

Later that afternoon it was time to leave Madge to spend some days further along the track with Jack and Sash, who were known locally as desert hermits. They would regularly duck into the one-corner-store town once a month for supplies and to get any messages. Pip and Dawn had run the corner-store for years, loving the remoteness and the quiet, but they were as garrulous as any I knew when someone popped in for a chat. They had put me in touch with Father Jack and Saint Sash. Everyone called them that, except Jack and Sash themselves. Nicknames given to them, as Pip said, "Out of respect. Never known people like it. Holy, that's what I call them. I don't know about God, but I know holy when I see it."

The sun was getting low when I saw them coming, the dust swirling around their feet; both with what reminded me of staffs, walking sticks whittled out of wood, and accompanied by a dingo-like dog at their heels, which I later found out was called Cuthbert, after the Celtic hermit who lived on Farne Island in the seventh century.

They were intensely warm and open as we greeted one another, asking question after question about who I was and where I was from, why I was here. I barely got a chance to find out about them, but I knew there would be time for that.

Introductions done, local news swapped, and the weather predicted, we left Pip and Dawn at the store. The air was now becoming distinctively cooler with the sun almost set, but I could still smell the warmth of the earth rising as we scuffed our way along the red dust road, back to their camp three kilometers away. Cuthbert kept sniffing my heels as if to find out what news I might have brought from other places and other dogs. I took the opportunity to make friends with him, and it seemed he was happy to have anyone pay attention to him. Soon he was walking by my heels and we had a kind of comfortable rapport.

We walked in silence, and my eyes strained to adjust to the dimming light. When we arrived, I set up my tent down the dry creek bed from their hut, unpacked my rucksack and shook out my old down sleeping bag. Tugging my jumper on against the desert evening chill I made my way over to their camp kitchen. The billy was on, the tea ready and mugs set out. They had received a handful of visitors over the past four years, they told me; folk who were hungry for silence and solitude and to find out ways of living that nurtured silence. Jack and Sash's own love for the Celtic monastic life had long been in their blood. Father Jack had left Australia to be part of an experimental monastic community in Scotland, where families, couples, and singles all lived a monastic rule of life similar to some of the early Celtic communities. That's where he had met Sash. The community had gone well until the media discovered them and "It was downhill from there," he told me. They clearly didn't want to go over that history. They had then come back together to Australia to explore beginning another community here, but instead found themselves drawn as a couple to a hermit lifestyle in the desert outback where they had lived for several years.

We settled around the fire with hot tea and Cuthbert lying by my elbow.

"You see this fire?" Father Jack reflected. "Listen to it, and look. It leaps with laughing and its flames turn their bodies round and round like dancing thieves as they steal away the night and the cold, heat them, mold them, shape them into warmth and the magic of a carnival of light. Sparks fly like a heated argument, and I love arguments." He paused for a while. I was keen to hear more from this storyteller.

He continued, "Out here I spend most of my time railing against the sun—she doesn't know when to stop broiling the earth down here. I often argue that if she turned herself down just a little in the heat of the day, she would allow the shadows to speak more invitingly and the ants wouldn't have to burrow so deep and we could grow more veggies. That would make us all happy. But she's pretty feisty and doesn't listen to my arguments. So I surrender (and that's a good word, by the way) and let myself unfurl into the heat and absorb her as part of me. And after a while—and you will find this too if you stay long enough—after a while you begin to accept this deep heat and she begins to softly massage her way through the pores of your skin; she moves in slowly and gently like stealth and takes you by surprise. You begin to feel at one with the heat and no longer fight her as if she were apart from you. She is you. And then you discover you are free to move around in the noonday sun, no arguments now, just a surrendered acceptance and agreement with her like an old married couple."

Sash chuckled over the rim of her mug, the steam catching the firelight as it hovered before her lips. She seemed much older than Jack. Her long grey hair had been rolled up into a soft bun at the back of her head, her nose was aquiline, and her high cheekbones made her seem strangely like Balthasar Denner's eighteenth-century *Portrait of an Old Woman* that I had been drawn to some time ago. Her wrinkles were expressive, and a knowing smile played at the corners of her mouth. I felt as if I had met Saint Sash already in that portrait. There was such a sense of safety about her. I knew straight away I could be myself, make any silly mistakes or ask anything stupid and I would be safe with her—safe from judgment, ridicule, needing to measure up.

Jack added a few more logs to the fire. His toothy grin was endearing as we sat listening to the fire pop, spark, and crackle its own language into the conversation. The glow on his face made the ridges and furrows deeper, like a richly ploughed field ready for sowing. His eyebrows were long and wispy with multiple mini-antennae, alert to sensing the shifts of weather and the drifts of wind, the beckoning of the desert oaks that told him scarce rains were on the way. Jack's eyebrows even seemed to move independently as he talked. His mouth had a sensitivity that spoke of a tender awareness as he chewed on an acacia sprig.

We gazed at the flames, forty thousand thieves at work clothed in intense orange and yellow and white sheens of fire-fabric with flashes of blue and green, flouncing and stretching, showing off like gypsies dancing in the palace of the desert.

I picked out from the fire a stick that was glowing. Lifting it up I spun it in the air and watched the circles of light run through the dark desert sky like neon writing. This is a place where you could spin poetry in the sky.

The sky. I let my eyes leave the fire and adjust to the darkness, which was filled with starlight. I felt I could touch it, soft, dark, and velvety like purple-blue violets. The sky looked like infinity; it smelt smoky-dark blue and of warm woody chestnuts. The stars and planets sang stronger than all of British musician Gustav Holst's compositions and sweeter than NASA's recordings of solar sounds. I opened my mouth and I could taste sparkling black shiraz, aged and otherworldly. No wonder the ancients thought this was heaven.

How many times had I heard someone bemoan the fact that God—whoever God was to them—just wasn't clear or understandable, and that they wished she would write in neon lights across the sky to assure them of her existence, or give guidance and tell them what to do. But wasn't *this* taste the taste of God, *this* smell, *this* touching of infinity with its infilling depth of presence and joy deeper than any neon-lit billboard happiness? This dripping black-sky grape juice that sets my mouth watering, my heart beating and my eyes wide awake to the Presence in the fire-warmed night air? So much more intimate an awakening and communion than some kind of external distant god using graffiti on a wall to guide us. But was this tasting of God "clear"? No. Understandable? No. But all my senses were touched and enveloped in this divine night blessing. Here was the opening of deep intimacy with Ultimacy.

This was Sky-God, Night-God, Infinite-Warm-Presence God. And Grandmother God was here too. She had accompanied me as I left Old

Madge, and was now settled down within me by the fire, a centered, earthy wisdom-companion. We sat together around that fire in companionable silence until late.

For the next several days I joined Jack and Sash in their largely silent rule of life with its rhythm of work and prayer. It included elements of the Rule written by Benedict of Nursia (480–550), with its two wings of prayer and work. They included *lectio divina* (holy reading) each morning, where we read aloud a sentence or two of Scripture and mulled over it silently, letting it sink down slowly over the hour from our head to our heart where it began to sing its own song. This was followed by work, which for Jack was chopping wood, mending some of the fencing, checking on their sheep with Cuthbert, and wood carving. For Sash it was their small experimental vegetable garden and continuing with her handweaving of wool scarves and wall hangings. She had three hand looms all with partially finished projects on the go.

Rhythms of Prayer

Lunch time began with an examen before eating. Jack described how they did this together each day. Sasha remarked that there were times when her examen had been so full, "And then you find you have had your fill and you don't have much room for lunch!"

I settled into this time to reflect on the details of the day, weighing my senses associated with each moment that called my attention and carried some tiny weight of significance. The examen can vary, but here I was focusing on the steps: first to be open to the Spirit's way of seeing my day; then to notice the things to be grateful for, followed by those elements that were life-giving. After this, the opportunity to note anything that needed to be released, and finally to receive again the unconditional love of God.

Sitting in the shade of silent companionship, I began to trace the nuanced moments of the day, following the pattern that the ancients suggested for this form of prayer. Opening my hands, I opened myself to the insight that Mothering Spirit would bring: a way of seeing that would go beyond my own habitual assumptions. The leaves rustled above me as I recalled the gifts from the day, "the gratitude moments" as some Jesuits refer to it: the first breezes of early morning, the single birdsong in the distance, the varied browns and rust colors in the bark. I receive these from the gracious hands of the Creator. Then I traced my day along the filigreed moments of the day that were energizing and consoling: Jack's knowing grin; Sash's small sayings that gave sustenance like the little desert raisins; and the sensing I had of the Divine walking with me. I drew these gifts from the day into myself as nourishment, savoring them. I then needed to move on to the next part of the examen: to retrace my steps and notice what were the niggles, the things that were draining, or the times my ego was at work. And then to let these go before God. Then I entered the still wonder of the unconditional love of Creator God.

After lunch was the much-needed rest in the heat of the day and while Sash and Jack retired to their hut, each afternoon I wandered off to sit under the shade of a tree up on the low ridge. From here I could see for miles and sometimes a slight breeze would speak to me of the Spirit moving. This was time to journal.

One afternoon, gazing out over the vast expanse of red dirt with trees, grasses, and sandstone rock the color of honeycomb, I became aware of a sense of lostness, which seemed to come like a dust cloud out of nowhere; a sense of unsureness of how to be with God. The desert seemed to mirror my own disorientation and barrenness. After such an affirming time with Old Madge, and the first few days here, I was taken aback when I felt myself begin to descend into a bit of a dip, which didn't take long to blow out into a hole. A big, black, vacuous hole. Where did this come from? I couldn't shake it off.

As the late afternoon sun started to sink, I sank with it. I wandered back to the kitchen to help with preparing the evening meal. I kept my experience to myself. I had no words to describe this "hole"; how do you describe nothingness? And how can nothingness actually at the same time feel like decimation? After the meal and washing-up, I meandered out toward my tent.

The night was clear but dark; the moon was not yet up. I found a tree in the riverbed and sat with my back up against it, trying to draw from it some solidness and strength to take away my querulous weakness and, yes, lostness. Where was Grandmother God now? Had it all been just a figment of my imagination? As the temperature dropped rapidly, it felt God was giving me the cold shoulder. Despite feeling cold, I wanted to wait for the moon to bring the light I didn't have.

For the next couple of days, I sagged liked a broken hammock hanging against that riverbed tree, which became my solace. At least here was something solid, sure, tangible. I knew all the scriptures that reassure us that God never leaves us or forsakes us (Heb 13:5), and that this God is the One in whom we live and move and have our being (Acts 17:28), without whom we would cease to exist; whose presence goes with us and in whom we will find rest (Exod 33:14). And I was also aware of Job's experience, and how the Bible speaks of the Hidden God (Isa 45:15)—hidden not because God plays games but because we go through seasons like the moon. Sometimes experiencing shadow, sometimes feeling in full sunlight, but no matter the season, the sun does not stop shining. However, simply knowing this wasn't giving me the hand-up I needed out of the deep suctioning darkness.

The silence felt like a drumming pressure on my ears, and yet at the same time the silence had an emptiness—almost a hollowness—to it. How does one manage the experience of apparent absence of this Eternal-Presence-God? It was a paradox boring a hole in my soul.

It became too burdensome to keep trying to be present to Cold-Shoulder-God, so I turned my attention to the riverbed gum tree. I began wondering how the dry creek bed supported such a huge gum tree. I knew that underground aquifers are most accessible from riverbeds as they are the lowest level of ground where water would gather. And even though the water is not visible, tree roots would reach many metres down to get as much water as possible.

Part of me wanted to think of this as a metaphor for my own situation, an encouragement to dig deep for sustenance. But I felt closer to Dante's depiction of souls trapped in gnarled and twisted trees. Only if the tree poured sap or "bled," according to Dante's *Inferno*, could the soul have a voice. I felt trapped and without a voice, unable to translate what was happening into some language I could understand. I wondered what would have to bleed to enable me to articulate a way forward.

The tree image prompted my memory of another desert retreat I had been on out near Kalgoorlie in Western Australia. There we were shown some of the fluted gimlet trees. Remarkably beautiful, their multi-based trunks were a rich orange that glowed distinctively in the late afternoon sun. If we put our ears up against the tree, and quietened ourselves, from time to time we could hear the sap running through the flutes in the trunk. In such a dry climate this was quite magical! And I remembered the retreat owner had described how he had used a gimlet branch to make a long shepherd's crook for a friend's ordination as bishop. I began reflecting on how I was sitting with my back up against this tree, and wondered: perhaps if I stand up, turn and put my ear to the trunk of the riverbed tree, I might then listen to this trapped soul of mine running like tree sap inside the tree. Would this tree guide me with its own shepherd's crook?

As I leaned against the tree, my head resting against the trunk listening, it dawned on me: this is exactly what Ignatius encourages in his "Rules for Discernment," which I have referred to so much in leading retreats and as a spiritual director. Now I needed to apply it to myself. First, I needed to acknowledge that I was in desolation and name it as such. And second, Ignatius says at such times to stand back and become an observer of ourselves when in desolation, knowing that we are more than this experience. The desolation I was experiencing after the feast of presence over the first few days was not atypical. Ignatius wrote a letter to one of his directees, Sr. Teresa Rejadell, speaking into her darkness. In it he describes desolation:

> He [the enemy] makes use of everything to vex us, and everything in the first lesson [consolation] is reversed. We find ourselves sad without knowing why. We cannot pray with devotion, or contemplate, nor even speak or hear of the things of God with any interior taste or relish. Not only this, but if he sees that we are weak and much humbled by these harmful thoughts, he goes on to suggest that we are entirely forgotten by God our Lord, and leads us to think that we are quite separated from God and that all that we have done and all that we desire to do is entirely worthless. He thus endeavors to bring us to a state of general discouragement.[3]

I began to reflect on my time so far. I began to see that I had so enjoyed the consolation with Old Madge and the first days with Jack and Sash, that I had actually begun to feel a sense of entitlement. That somehow, even though part of me knew without a doubt it was sheer gift, there was another part of me that was taking credit for it, assuming it was because of my spirituality; and that in some way I was the one controlling this experience of grace. And this "demand" was alienating me from the true Presence. This was the necessary bleeding or bloodletting as my soul was being released, slowly, into voicing its way forward.

I turned again, this time to simply lie prostrate under the tree on the blood-red sand, my arms outstretched and my hands open to this Absent God who accompanies me, an ethereal guide in the desert. God remained "absent," but I had a great sense of shalom along with timelessness—a rightness in the dark that all would be well and I could simply "be" in the presence of absence, present to a Silence of Nothingness.

The Wisdom of a Dragon

Some days later, it was the mid-afternoon time for meditation. Jack was adamant that I should only join them if I wanted to, which I did. In the afternoon prayers they used *visio divina*, or divine seeing, a time of silent meditation on something visual that allowed for an encounter with the Divine. The focus can be whatever visually draws interest—anything in the

---

3. Endean, "Discerning behind the Rules," 41.

landscape or even the most ordinary thing such as a chair or a window. We were each to choose our own image to focus on.

"There may be times when you need to go to the very thing that repels you," said Sash over a coffee. "Don't always go to the beautiful things. The ugly or repulsive may have the deepest wisdom for you—uncomfortable, perhaps, but there will be something for you there. Behold it with the eyes of your heart, and by that, I mean take in every aspect of it—what you see, what you feel, what you smell, and what you sense—watch for this particularly." She topped up my mug, as if she knew I would need the extra caffeine hit for what was coming.

She continued, "It may be a sense of the sacred, of presence, of absence, of agitation, repulsion. Speak with it, ask its history, and let it tell you its story. And whatever it is, let it tell you what you need to hear. Then ruminate on that, not with your head or your mind, but with your soul, your very gut." I nodded.

"This is where deep change in us happens. Transformation of our minds changes our thinking; transformation at a gut level changes our behavior." She looked at me steadily and began collecting the mugs.

For some reason I felt discouraged. My immediate desire was to find something beautiful to ponder on. That was so much easier, so much more attractive and more constructive, surely? I ambled off down the dry creek bed. Who knows when it had last seen water? Yet it held such profound beauty—the stately tall gum trees, with patterned bark and sweeping branches full of multicolored leaves. If I stood so the sun shone through them, they became translucent—red, rust, dark and light greens, brown, orange, with little bright-green gum nuts hanging in bunches.

I walked on, half-looking for the unattractive thing that I was meant to find. I scrambled up the ledge of the riverbank and started to walk through the grasses, which were surprisingly dense. And there I found it, or it found me, by stabbing my legs through my sock and jeans, stopping me in my tracks. Spinifex grass! Spiky, harsh, unfriendly, and definitely unattractive. Sitting down to begin the meditation was going to be the challenge. Round and around I turned like Cuthbert trying to settle on a space to rest without getting speared again. Finally, I settled and began to rest my eyes on the rounded tussocks of grass in front of me.

I found out later that it was not spinifex, which is more a coastal species, but rather triodia, a desert species that covers around a quarter of Australia's land surface. So not only was it ugly, it was common too. But with roots extending down to depths of four metres into the sand, and with the ability to thrive on almost no nutrition, this grass's indomitable resilience is the reason given as to why Australian deserts are not barren like most of the Sahara. The Aboriginal people crushed the stems to retrieve the resin, which is like an extremely strong glue. So, there are some hidden gems in this porcupine grass!

I checked my watch so that I knew exactly when the hour would be up and I could be up and out of there. I took a few deep breaths and my body called me back to this pinprick of time, this sharp pointy moment suspended on the tip of a blade of grass. Was this my tipping point? My time to let myself be pierced by the grace of this dry desert exercise?

The grass was grey, quite a boring grey. There were long tubular blades—spear-like needles that sprayed out from the rounded base, some looked like very tiny threading needles, and others reaching up about a metre high. Halfway down each one there seemed to be one or two spikes protruding like arms at right angles, again each with spear-like tips. I was sure at least one of those had my blood on it! The dense pincushion base was made up of dark-green softer blades, and I began to notice a furry woolliness around the bottom of the blades.

I reached out to feel one, careful not to get stabbed again, and my fingers closed on a delicate cottony fleece-like coating. As I looked closer, it was no longer just a dull grey but rather its coloring graded from dark lavender to snowy white. Almost delicate—and I hadn't seen it before at all. A protection for its base? Or a collector of rare water? As I pulled my hand away I heard a rustle of movement behind me. Then nothing. Another rustle, and again nothing. Some little critter was paying a visit, but I couldn't see it. I slowly and quietly looked around. I noticed that some of the hummocks of grass had died out in the middle, forming doughnut rings. And in the center of the grass doughnut behind me I spotted it! It had already spotted me.

I had seen these before, so knew it was a thorny dragon lizard, but I had never been so close to one, nor had I given myself the time to simply look, and I reminded myself this was after all *visio divina*, so I had permission to stay as long as I wanted. It was quite stunning with its prickliness and stripes of earthy colors. I had heard that thorny dragon lizards collected water by rubbing their bodies against desert grasses so the microdrops of dew run down hygroscopic grooves leading right to the corners of their mouth.

His body was covered with scales and rows of thorny horns. The tail, prickly and about as long as his body, was pointing straight upwards, as if to say, I am one of the stalks of grass, so please ignore me. On the back of his neck was a large thorny lump—a false head to trick any predator. Hardly an object of beauty. Only as big as my hand, he was eyeing me, swaying on his thorny haunches. I quietly sat down to gaze on this ostentatious dwarf dragon. His jaw was rotating as if chewing on some unseen thoughts he was having, ruminating in his blue mouth about the options before him. A slow mover, I knew and he knew that running would get him nowhere, so we silently agreed to watch one another. And so we did. What are you teaching me, I thought? What's your story, and what of the Divine are you showing me?

We didn't have words, but we had a language: we shared the silence, the heat, the gazing at one another, the swaying—I was dancing with my dragon in time with time itself. Almost hypnotized, I wondered if this was the beholding that Sash had spoken of, only I felt the dragon was beholding me too. What did he see?

I thought of some of the dragons I had known: Tolkien's Smaug, who cried out, "I am death" as he headed out to destroy with fire breath; Puff the Magic Dragon of my childhood; the headmistress of my high school, whose breath might well have had a match put to it. And then of course there was my own inner dragon created by me as a defence against the world. Not a helpful, happy dragon, but not a big one either. A nuisance really, getting in the way of healthy choices. Could this little scaly dragon lizard have some helpful wisdom for the thorny dragon in my life?

The dragon lizard stopped swaying and became stock still, without taking his eyes off me. What concentration and focus—he could teach a meditation class! The silence had its own sounds—a muted bird-cry far off, the hazy sound of grass rubbing grass as the breeze flowed through, and the sound of my own heart beating a tune in my ears. His mouth was still chewing, moving as if he was savoring something. In the stillness I imagined I could even faintly hear the sounds of his little mouth. Perhaps he was feasting on a tiny drop of water that he had found?

How often do I race on and not savor tiny drops of grace I have been given, tiny drops of water that give life? In my rush and race to be part of the world that moves so fast, I am in danger of despising the little things, and committing such a blasphemy against the beauty of life, and consequently begin to bury myself in the coffin of busyness. What a deathly way to live: a true dragon of death to be feared, and yet how insidiously and stealthily it has crept into my world. This indeed was my lizard's teaching to me—take the time to relish the richness of the little things in life. I needed to take slow, languorous sips of grace as you would aged wine, letting the taste flow fruitfully, mingling with every morsel of doubt and fear, joy and laughter, permeating my whole being.

His whole layer of skin, the biggest organ of the lizard dragon, is designed to bring the most minute drops of water to his mouth for survival. I smiled admiringly at this little dragon so intricately designed to live well in harsh climates. Could I not ready my whole skin, all the pores of my being to receive, funnel, and drink in minute droplets of graced moments?

How alive and life-giving that would be. This was a divine encounter—God using this little hand-sized lizard to show me what it means to stop, savor, and receive life from the smallest of things. I needed to hear this. My whole body began to relax into the heat and the company of the little dragon; more shoulder to shoulder than face to face; the slight breeze, a faint birdcall and the silence. Thoughts, sounds, and senses gave way to a deep interior silence which settled inside; a spaciousness opened within me, lowering me into my very center where a slow burn of transformation took place. Unaware of my surroundings, and even of my breathing, it seemed as if I entered a timelessness, a sense of Presence that only silence can describe. A oneness with the Divine that came unbeckoned. I stayed long in that place, until I became conscious of a slight breeze touching the grasses, calling my senses back to awareness.

When good wine and whiskey age in great oak barrels, there is a shimmer sometimes seen around the horizon of the wood. This is called angels' breath or angels' share, and is the evaporation of distilled spirits coming through the pores of the wood. Maybe my skin will do both—receive the goodness from life, let it transform me and age me well, and then give it back to neighbors and the world in angels' breath, in the kind of hospitality that Sash and Jack offered so spaciously. The kind of hospitality that this little dragon gave so humbly. I had a choice—live a life that shares the fire of dragon's breath or live a life that shares the spirited angels' breath.

The wind had picked up further and the sun was dropping fast. Amazingly, my little dragon was still there, and I was so reluctant to leave. I feared there might be more wisdom and I would miss out if I left too soon. But no, this was enough—more than enough. I was satiated. It was time for me to ruminate on these droplets.

Following the example of Francis of Assisi, I thanked the lizard for our time together and made my way back to the camp. That night, I watched the sunset washing the sky with liquid amber. I savored the nectar of the last few days. I was learning how to listen to the language of fire and to see with soft eyes what at first was so unappealing.

Honey is known for its sweetness, but in the ancient Near East it was used for healing, cooking, and mixing with wine. It was rare, and sometimes given as a gift. Even manna, the bread from heaven given to the Israelites, was said to taste like honey. I reflected on my time with Old Madge, on her wisdom, and how she introduced me to the wild desert-honey taste of the honeypot ants. That was manna for me—a feasting on all Madge had to show me. I recalled the hole I had buried myself in under the tree and the slow life that returned. And I could still visualize my thorny dragon nestled in the doughnut of needle grass—grass and dragon together in their sharp spikiness, together in their initial ugliness, together making a home in the desert and each giving their different valuable gifts to those who take the time to see with the eyes of the heart.

REFLECTION

Silent Voices of the Desert

Many of the early mystics and desert fathers and mothers fled to the desert, not as a place of escape, but as a place of confrontation with their own inner demons and of deep encounter with the living God. Their desire was to be honed in authenticity and conformed to the image of God. In a world where mendaciousness is so often rewarded, there is a deep craving for authenticity. Through the silences of deserts, God speaks, reaching into the depths of our souls. Estelle Frankel, a spiritual director and teacher of Jewish mysticism, notes that "the Hebrew word for speech, *dibbur*, has the same root (*dalet-bet-resh*) as the word for desert, or midbar. In the silence of the midbar of Sinai, the divine dibbur is heard—a fact that suggests that authentic speech is that which flows from its source in silence."[4]

Silence both enables us to hear God speaking in the "sheer silence" as Elijah did (1 Kgs 19), and to cultivate a dialogue between our interior silences and God of the Great Silence. Just as human voices have different qualities, so too silences have different textures. We can be engaged in the desert by silences of varied shades, in the same way light variations catch our attention due to different angles of the sun, or particles in the atmosphere. The French writer Antoine de Saint-Exupéry, when discussing the beauty of the desert with the Little Prince, remarks, "I have always loved the desert. One sits down on a desert sand dune, sees nothing, hears nothing. Yet through the silence something throbs, and gleams."[5] Some silences can indeed have voices that throb and gleam, while others can sound oppressive, vacuous, or death-dealing. Remaining open to receive all the nuanced languages of the desert silences, absorbing the wondrous silences, and facing those silences that frighten us, allows the desert to be our teacher, guiding us into authenticity.

The God of all exodus movements, who leads us through our wanderings in the desert, also provides manna for us. How extraordinary to find honey in a desert, and especially within an ant! Manna in the desert. Honey

---

4. Frankel, *Sacred Therapy*, section: "Emotional Expressiveness as Redemptive," para. 4, 121–22.

5. De Saint-Exupéry and Howard, *Little Prince*, 75.

is found throughout the Bible, often as a metaphor, and is used to suggest exuberant delight and sweetness, at the same time as referring to the word of God and to wisdom. Perhaps one of the best-known references is found in Psalm 19:9–10, "The ordinances of the LORD are true and righteous altogether. More to be desired are they than gold, even much fine gold; sweeter also than honey, and drippings of the honeycomb." And in some medieval mystical prayers, Christ is referred to as "the Honeycomb." The association of honey with a transcendent goodness that can be tasted is strong. It is also important to note that honey may well be prevalent and easy to access at any supermarket where we live, but in some parts of the ancient Near East it was a luxury, saved for special occasions. It is something desirable and needs to be sought. In some Judaic traditions, at the start of children's education honey was dripped on their first page as a prayer that their process of learning would always be sweet to them. Perhaps we need to look out for drips of honey forming on our journals, rich gifts to relish slowly like dragon's mead.

Somewhat like Hagar, we can sit in the desert wailing and bereft, and yet right nearby Hagar was a well, which the angel pointed out to her (Gen 21). She hadn't been able to see it—perhaps her tears blurred her vision. It became an epiphany for her. Often what we most need is right near us. One of the many gifts those who live close to the land offer us all is their knowledge of how to survive in the desert, and just how much food and water can be found that is not easily visible to most urban-dwellers. Many parts of the mulga tree that we had been sitting under are edible: parts of the bark can be used for gum, the seeds (a low-glycemic starch) for flour, the cooked flowers for eating. So much in one plant. What at first feels to be an inhospitable and impoverished landscape becomes a place of plenty. Not all deserts have such abundance, but in all deserts we need eyes to see and ears to hear: a receptivity of spirit to notice the food that is there before us.

The image of Grandmother God was a remarkable burst of honey-sweetness as a fresh image of God. It is such a slow process not only for ourselves but also for the church as a whole to fully acknowledge how male images and masculine God-language is not only confining for all of us, but also harmful for many. The Bible is brimming with such rich varieties of images and metaphors for God, demonstrating that God is neither male nor female, masculine nor feminine, and has no physical body but comes to us in ways we can apprehend. Some of those might be through other people or through gender-neutral images such as Rock or Living Water. Just as God came to me that day through Old Madge, and God came to Hagar, prompting her to name God as "the God Who Sees Me" in her silent desert, so God comes to us and gives us courage to name God from our own authentic encounters.

"We are a people of memory," writes the Carmelite theologian and author Constance Fitzgerald. She speaks of how dwelling prayerfully in deep silence enables "a kind of unravelling" of memory to occur in such a way that the memories are not suppressed or obliterated, but instead are "uncoupled from the self. . . . In a mysterious way there is a cutting off of both past and memory that is inimical to one's personhood."[6] God's Spirit helps us by honing wholesome ways of being in relation to our past, and creating a bank of new life-giving images and memories that we can savor.

Desert Hospitality

Some years ago, I visited the St. Macarius desert monastery, founded in 360 CE in Egypt's Wadi El Natrun, about ninety kilometers west of Cairo. One of the monks there described how each monk discerned the degree to which they would live in silence. Some had less silence, and were drawn to being involved in the hospitality of visitors; other monks among them lived more as hermits, with extremely little social interaction. Here was such a gracious recognition that there is no "one size fits all" with regard to silence, rather we are each called to different degrees of silence. The monks believed that in faithfully following their calling into silence and contemplative prayer, they were empowered to be part of transformative processes politically, socially, and environmentally. John Chryssavgis, a Greek Orthodox minister and author, also points out this link between silence and a compassionate response to the world around us. He notes that unless we tend to the deserts and wastelands within, we will not have the wisdom or compassionate presence to bring peace to our own relationships nor know how to prevent the world around us becoming wastelands.[7]

Jack and Sash had responded to a deep interior longing to settle in the desert because above all they wanted to center their lives on the Divine and to be a sign to others of the compassionate presence of God. Some do this in the cities, they were doing it here in the desert. They could be seen as eccentric, yet the description of "eccentric" seems to hold a negative judgment within it. However, reflecting on the unusual vocations of the desert mothers and fathers, Chryssavgis remarks, "eccentricity means moving the center, re-centering the world on God."[8] It was this recentering that Jesus was demonstrating to the disciples. In response to their arguing about who was the greatest among them, Jesus—creating a living parable—draws a small

6. Fitzgerald, "From Impasse to Prophetic Hope," 23.

7. Chryssavgis, *In the Heart of the Desert.*

8. Chryssavgis, *In the Heart of the Desert,* ch. 14, para. 16.

child to himself and points out that it is the posture of hospitality towards others and towards God that defines greatness (Matt 18:2–5).

Time spent in the desert is an opportunity for readjusting our prayer compass and recentering ourselves and our way of living on God. To take the time to do desert work with God can be seen as a waste of time, countercultural, eccentric, and unnecessary. Yet our materialistic throwaway lifestyles sow destruction both in the environment around us and also interiorly. And so we need the silence that "does the deep work that speech cannot accomplish,"[9] and we need to risk becoming an eccentric. It is sobering that in the 1800s, John Stuart Mill was lamenting the pressures of conformity in society, to its own demise:

> Eccentricity has always abounded when and where strength of character has abounded; and the amount of eccentricity in a society has generally been proportional to the amount of genius, mental vigour, and moral courage which it contained. That so few now dare to be eccentric, marks the chief danger of the time.[10]

And so, in some ways not unlike Russia's "Holy Fools," Jack and Sash together are a living parable: something to ponder upon, and allow to chip away like a pickaxe at our own assumptions and lifestyle. Do we center our lives too much around fears associated with ambition, acclamation, recognition, and achievement? How many of us return continually to the question: Am I enough? Am I relevant enough? Brueggemann speaks about our theology of scarcity, where we so often fear that not only are *we* not enough, but also that God's love might not be enough.[11] Through his commentary on Israel's fear-based assumptions of scarcity, he alerts us to the fact that this God of infinite love invites us out of fearful wanderings into a theology of abundance. Each time we go into the desert, the emptiness can help us begin again, emptying our hands and ourselves of all the clutter and baggage we carry. There is no hurry in the desert; there are no trains to catch, people to see, meetings to attend, to-do lists to complete. Spending time in the desert can enable stillness to enter us by osmosis, and together with the vastness of the sky recalibrate our center. The desert is a powerful teacher of priorities.

9. Bennett, "Endangered Habitat," 67.
10. Mill, *On Liberty*, ch. 3, para. 13.
11. Brueggemann, "Liturgy of Abundance."

Oscillating in Prayer

Simone Weil, writing in the 1930s, reflected on how those who do not have God in themselves cannot feel God's absence.[12] We can experience great warmth and consolation and then without apparent reason (or sometimes we can identify a trigger), we can plummet into what feels to be a darkness and even an absence of the God we were previously so intimate with.

These are natural movements in the rhythms of prayer, especially when we are spending a dedicated few days or longer to pray. It can intensify the prayer experience. So rhythms of prayer practices—now examen, now *lectio divina*—can also have their counterpoints of rhythms of experience: now full, now empty; now a lightness of being, now a heavy darkness; now close, now far; now consolation, now desolation; now kataphatic, now apophatic. And little of it is within our control. "The passionate desire for God is one whose fulfillment exacts the most radical undoing of self; it is a journey marked by true joy but also darkness and obscurity; it is a commitment that asks everything, and takes all."[13] Oscillations between joy and darkness, consolation and desolation, are an integral part of the cartography of the desert and indeed of our spirituality. It is normal to experience this, but it is important too to have a skilled companion who has dwelled in deserts themselves to be a guide alongside you.

There are no maps for most deserts. They are uncharted territory to all except those who live there. The great dictum attributed to the Polish-born American semanticist and philosopher Alfred Korzybski (1879–1950), that the map is not the territory,[14] can be consoling—it doesn't matter that there are huge areas with no paths or tracks, no signposts or directions. It is about our own experience. Maps by definition always need to reduce the scale of the territory, and are forever therefore an abstraction. But a 1:1 scale is the territory itself, leaving abstraction behind and allowing our own personal encounter to occur, the one to One, and also between us and the land. We would never find "lost" written on a map, but in the desert we can embrace our lostness—lost is a place too. A valid place to be, necessary even, if something new is to come.

Times of consolation and intimacy with God are gifts of grace and joy in the love of God. A feast of Presence from God. When we are given these gifts, we need to store them in our memory banks, and continue to savor them. Ignatius constantly reminds us that during such times we are to

---

12. Weil, *Gravity and Grace.*
13. Fitzgerald, "Carmelite Beatitudes," no page number.
14. Korzybski, *Selections from Science and Sanity.*

humbly acknowledge this gracious outpouring of God and reflect that soon there will be a trial and possible desolation. The spiritual life is not one long honeymoon filled only with light. Far from glorifying suffering, we tenaciously hold on to the fact that "suffering produces endurance, and endurance produces character, and character produces hope, and hope does not disappoint us, because God's love has been poured into our hearts through the Holy Spirit that has been given to us" (Rom 5:3–5). Our prayer journey can take us from great consolation, to a slow descent, and then into enervation, trapped and almost with a sense of no longer dwelling in silence, but having been silenced, without language or voice to transpose this chaos into some form of order or tranquillity. A desolation. Then finally, through prompting by this absent God, prayer can change from something we are doing, to a posture of surrendered being, and we begin to emerge into the light again.

We are to ready ourselves for these fluctuations and be able to refer to times of spiritual consolation when desolation overwhelms us. The Jesuit author Jules J. Toner suggests a helpful posture in such circumstances:

> I set myself-in-desolation apart from myself-reflecting-on-myself-in-desolation. . . . By doing this, I have made space in my consciousness for something besides desolation with its causes and consequences. In that space I can now reconnoitre, manoeuvre my attention and reason and will, and thus attack and weaken or even destroy the sources of desolation.[15]

Ignatius's advice is to stand back and notice that we are in desolation, as an observer stands back and notices anger rising. We are then not to "pay any attention to the unpleasant impressions caused in us, and hope patiently for the consolation of the Lord."[16] It is easier said than done, to be able to stand back and notice, *and* to do it without self-judgment or condemnation.

Listening to the Book of Nature

God is walking everywhere, incognito, yet communicating with us through all things. Moses spent his time in the desert day after day. Such desert silence enabled him to be watchful and alert to a slightly unusual happening in the corner of his eye: a smoldering bush (Exod 3). He was awake to the small things that could be easily missed. He then chose to draw near to it. He had the inclination as well as the time and spaciousness to do that. This

15. Toner, *Commentary on Saint Ignatius' Rules*, 151.

16. Endean, "Discerning behind the Rules," 41.

too, is one of the gifts of the desert: the spacious unhurriedness that opens possibilities such as being addressed by the great "I AM" through the bush. I was able to draw on this unhurried spaciousness to notice the little thing on the periphery—the dragon lizard. This was my "burning bush."

It seems Moses heard an audible voice. God has many ways to communicate with us, and some of these are languages, silence being one of them. The contemporary American poet Mary Oliver (1935–2019) shows us, through her poetry, a way of listening into and conversing with nature and, in order to this, she constantly reminds us we need to take time to be attentive. To wait. And German theologian Jutta Koslowski writes of how as we wait patiently, we begin to recognize that silence is a language God uses to call out other voices and languages, those of the environment as well as our own inner voice.[17] She goes on to say that in the depth of mystical experiences, these voices join as one voice. Silence then deepens the consciousness and "tunes it with the mystery dimension of the Divine and resonates with the divine presence in the world."[18]

And we encounter God through becoming attentive and beholding in wonder little-known saints, the trees, grasses, riverbeds, and the humblest and most exquisite of creatures, such as the honeypot ant and the dragon lizard. As we listen in to the wisdom all this strange and magnificent world has for us, we hear the Creator's voice, and are drawn into relishing a honeyed feast with God.

PONDERING YOUR OWN EXPERIENCES

- "Yes, she embodied Grandmother God to me that day." What images do you have of God that are helpful or unhelpful? Perhaps there are people you have encountered who may have opened your eyes to the Divine in new ways. How do you want to build on that? What role might silence have for you on that journey?

- "Eccentricity means moving the center, re-centering the world on God." Cultivating a contemplative life means we need to be countercultural and make space for the work that only prayerful silence can do in our lives. What have been your experiences of silence? Some of these might have been voluntarily entered into or where you have found yourself immersed not by your own choice into silence. What wisdom have you received from those times?

17. Koslowski, "Mother I Hear Your Heartbeat."
18. Painadath, "Transforming Power of Contemplative Silence," 33.

- "But wasn't *this* taste the taste of God, *this* smell, *this* touching of infinity with its infilling depth of presence and joy deeper than any neon-lit billboard happiness? This dripping black-sky grape juice that sets my mouth watering . . . ." What tastes, smells, touches of the Divine have you been aware of? How can you become more intimate in these ways with God?

- "Some silences can indeed . . . throb and gleam, while others can sound oppressive, vacuous, or death-dealing." How do we relate to the very different characters of such silences? How would you describe the characteristics of some of the silences you have experienced? How does God use the language of silence in your relationship? Or how would you *like* God to use this language with you?

- "We would never find 'lost' written on a map, but in the desert we can embrace our lostness—lost is a place too. A valid place to be, necessary even, if something new is to come." We often try to scurry out of lostness too quickly, before it is able to season us and set us on a new and maybe unexpected path. What do you do when you find yourself in the place called "Lost"? How do you unpack the meaning of silence as it speaks to you in that situation?

- What encounters with God have you experienced through nature? What have been your "burning bushes"? How would you like to treasure these: perhaps writing them as a story for family members, or as a poem, psalm, or liturgy; planting a symbolic seed in your garden, or creating something with your own hands?

FOR FURTHER ENGAGEMENT

Deserts: Internal and External

As we enter the desert, one of the most common experiences is we begin to see how the desert landscape around us reflects our own interior deserts. In the RSV Bible translation, the word "wilderness" or desert occurs 245 times in the Old Testament and thirty-five times in the New, but there are different types of wildernesses, not all of them hot and dry. All of them, however, are places where God teaches the people about reliance, not on themselves, but on the Divine. It is a place of new beginnings in the refining fire of the heat. In Israel's experience, there was grumbling and defiance, but it was also a time of intimate dependency: "I remember the devotion of your youth, your love as a bride, how you followed me into the wilderness, in a land not sown" (Jer 2:2). And for Jesus it was a place where he was confronted with temptation, yet also wilderness areas were places he would go for prayer and solitude.

The silence in the desert can be disorienting. I read some time ago of a couple who went on their honeymoon to a desert. As they walked across the top of one of the dunes, the husband decided to descend down one side, and the wife down the opposite side, with the dune separating them. When they each tried to call out to the other, their voices were simply absorbed into the dune. The only way they could make contact again was to physically find each other.

A desert is a place where old ways of solving problems often don't work—it is a different world, a place of different sound language, a place where we are reduced to utter dependence on the Living God. One of the desert fathers, Abba Poemen, said, "Vigilance, self-knowledge, and discernment; these are the guides of the soul. . . . To throw yourself before God, not to measure your progress, to leave behind all self-will; these are the instruments for the work of the soul."[19]

The desert has so much to teach us, whether it is our own internal desert or a physical external desert. Both deserve our attention. Pope Francis reminds us that external deserts in the world are growing, because the internal deserts have not been addressed and as a result have become so expansive.[20]

The deserts within our inner geography as a society can be vast. External and internal deserts are twin deserts. And as we encounter such desolation in our neighbors, we too can walk alongside them on the long road as the Spirit hovers over their chaos ready to bring light and goodness. The psalmist offers comfort in such a scenario, saying, "For it was you who formed my inward parts; you knit me together in my mother's womb" (Ps 139:13). And Laird comments, "God is the knitter for whom there are no dropped stitches, . . . a Presence likewise so simple as to manifest as absence, as both before and after, both within and without."[21]

Shifting Images

It is worth remembering that the biblical writers use metaphors for a reason: not simply to use colorful language but to capture a mountain of meaning in the seedpod of a word. Metaphors and parables require the

19. Ward, *Sayings of the Desert Fathers*, 35–36.

20. Pope Francis, "*Laudato Si*," no page number.

21. Laird, *Ocean of Light*, 59.

deliberate engagement of our imaginations, and are to be afforded the time and space to open out to us, like the flower that needs the right environment to blossom and let its fragrance affect us. Or the thorny dragon lizard that has so many lessons for us if we would only take the time to listen as the Spirit within unfolds to us the mysteries held in the details of its anatomy and lifestyle. Metaphors are a form of poetic language that is best understood not through tackling it with our rational minds, but in letting it unfold within us.

In the same way, metaphors are used to describe the Divine who is beyond description and impossible to confine to a single image. Biblical writers recorded different images of God, depending on what the Divine was revealing to them. As referred to above, Hagar called God "the One Who Sees Me," named as a result of her experience with God's very moving intervention. Chittister points out that "to the psalmist, God is a midwife; to Isaiah a comforting mother; in Exodus, the ultimate Being; in Haggai, a wife."[22] Other metaphors include references to the Divine as a mother hen, an eagle, living water, shelter, shield, and potter.

But there is for many an "undoing" that occurs as we learn to let go of past images and names for God in order for the new Hagar-like revelation of God to take root within us. For some this "unravelling" involves the letting go of images that have served us well enough to this point, but cannot be reconciled with our current life experiences. For others, this is an unravelling of previous destructive images of God that have impacted a person's identity and sense of self, and can be a very dark and liminal experience. This has been found to be particularly true of many women's experiences, to the point where theologian and contemplative scholar Beverly Lanzetta— as a result of her research—refers to this path throughout her book as *via feminina*,[23] and relates this to Teresa of Avila's movements of prayer.

Fitzgerald treats this painful journey with depth and sensitivity, as she relates the *via feminina* to John of the Cross's dark night where purification of memory takes place. She describes this process as being a form of *kenosis*, of self-emptying, that strips a person of all her previously firmly held beliefs of herself—some healthier than others—but all in need of revision as she deepens her contemplative life in God. There is also a mystical element to this: "Because this radical emptying out of woman's constructed selfhood is so profoundly united with the *kenosis* of Jesus, this dispossession in the feminine memory effects a solidarity that reaches far beyond the personal into the communal, into the souls of all women; then deeply into the human

22. Chittister, *In Search of Belief*, 25.
23. Lanzetta, *Radical Wisdom*.

spirit."[24] Our image of God is a key factor in how we view and relate to ourselves, our loved ones, our neighbors, and the world.

Kathleen Fischer, author and spiritual director, encourages us all to go deeper into contemplative prayer and there to trust our imaginations and our experiences of God. She refers to Teresa of Avila who trusts her encounters with God, allowing metaphors to arise, such as the depiction of her soul as a palace with crystal walls, and God as a bright diamond in the heart of the palace.[25] Images, metaphors, and symbols offer us a kataphatic way in prayer. And when we move beyond images into Presence, we find ourselves on the apophatic path of prayer. The one can lead to the other and, as Fischer says, these "intersect and converge in most of our spiritual lives."[26] Images disclose only some aspects of the Divine as no single image can contain God.

Consolation and Desolation

Ignatius describes consolation: "Sometimes my heart would feel as though it were overflowing with joy, such lightness, freedom, and consolation were in it. . . . Sometimes my eyes brimmed over with tears of thankfulness to God."[27] Consolation can be the wonder that one experiences at the beauty of a sunset, or a child playing, or an insight into the word of God; it can also be what is called "consolation without cause," meaning there is no apparent reason or cause for such an overflowing sense of abundance and blessing. It comes as a gift of grace.

But it is necessary to dig deeper into the concept of consolation, as there are two types and it is crucial to discern which we are experiencing. General consolation can refer to any feeling of contentment, joy, and peace, but does not have an impact on our relationship with God. But *spiritual* consolation, according to Ignatius, is where this experience then touches into our life of faith and our relationship with the Divine. All feelings of goodness come as gifts from the Creator, but in the context of prayer and with some reflection, what began as general consolation can become spiritual consolation as we allow it to affect our inner life with the Beloved. Gallagher gives a wonderful example of this from Thérèse of Lisieux.

Thérèse was visiting her sister and as she entered the garden she saw a hen under a tree protecting her little chicks under her wings. At first Thérèse

24. Fitzgerald, "From Impasse to Prophetic Hope," 29.

25. Fischer, *Women at the Well.*

26. Fischer, *Women at the Well,* 63.

27. Gallagher, *Discernment of Spirits,* ch. 3, para. 1.

found this charming and delightful. And then it suddenly dawned on her
that this was God speaking to her.

> A process of thought and affectivity gradually develops . . . as the
> scriptural understanding of this scene unfolds in her thoughts,
> Therese's heart turns to God in joy and tears begin to fall. . . .
> Then a further step takes place in this interior process, Therese
> has already progressed from the sight before her in the garden to
> a *general* teaching in Scripture; now she moves from this general
> teaching in Scripture to an awareness of how that teaching il-
> luminates her *personal* life: "All through my life, this is what he
> has done *for me!* He has hidden me totally under his wings." At
> this point she is too affected even to speak and tears well up.[28]

The role and value of reflection is illustrated well here. We can become
experience-rich: enjoying many wonderful gifts, but they do not transform
our relationship in God unless we reflect upon them, relish them, and allow them to become *spiritual* consolation. Not everything needs to progress
to this, but if we live a contemplative life, we will become attuned to such
possibilities and, where possible, in prayerful attentiveness will allow this
transformative work of the Spirit to occur.

Spiritual desolation is defined as "darkness of soul, disturbance in it,
movement to low and earthly things, disquiet from agitations and temptations, moving to lack of confidence, without hope, without love, finding
oneself totally slothful, tepid, sad, and, as if separated from one's Creator
and Lord."[29] Many of us experience bouts of general desolation from time
to time, but it becomes spiritual desolation when it impacts on our relationship with God. It is important at this point to be aware of the difference
between depression and desolation. It is beyond the scope of this chapter to
discuss this, but it is important to note that they are not the same, and if it is
depression then some professional care may be necessary.

Ignatius has guidelines for us when we find ourselves in desolation. The
scholarly and careful work by Toner (1982) is extremely instructive in out-
lining all of Ignatius's "Rules for Discernment," and discusses the guidelines
given by Ignatius in detail. Suffice it to say, consolation and desolation are
normal and expected parts of our spiritual journeys. And the assistance of
a spiritual director in helping discern these interior movements of the Spirit
can be invaluable to anyone yearning to grow closer to the heart of Love.

28. Gallagher, *Discernment of Spirits*, ch. 3, section: "A Specifically Spiritual Consolation," paras. 11–13.

29. Gallagher, *Discernment of Spirits*, Introduction, section: "The Text of the Rules,"
para. 5.

One of the desert sayings by Amma Syncletica sums up this journeying: "In the beginning there is struggle and a lot of work for those who come near to God. But after that there is indescribable joy. It is just like building a fire: at first it is smoky and your eyes water, but later you get the desired result. Thus, we ought to light the divine fire in ourselves with tears and effort."[30] Far from a place of escape, the desert is a place of encounter with God, with oneself, and with creation. A place to savor and relish—as difficult as they sometimes may be—the transformative gifts of the Spirit.

30. Elder, *Embracing the Spirit Within*, 224.

4

Tikkun Olam: Repairing Silence

"We cannot live in a world that is not our own, in a world that is interpreted for us by others. An interpreted world is not a home. Part of the terror is to take back our own listening, to use our own voice, to see our own light," declares Hildegard of Bingen. "Dare to declare who you are. It is not far from the shores of silence to the boundaries of speech. The path is not long, but the way is deep. You must not only walk there; you must be prepared to leap."[1]

In each chapter of this book, I have entered into a different silence. In this chapter I enter into the apocryphal book of Susanna as a way of healing some of the forced silences of women in the biblical and Christian traditions. Hildegard of Bingen (1098–1179), a remarkable reformer of monasteries and of theologies and now referred to as a doctor of the church, knew what it was to live in a society where women were silenced and did not have a voice. Her words above are sage advice, and in her own life she demonstrated what it meant to risk the path of using her voice and sharing her light. So I take the leap, entering into Susanna's silence, and I do so through

1. Hildegard of Bingen, quoted in Boden, *In the Hand of God*, para. 4.

the Jewish art of midrash. It is an imaginative retelling, rewriting Susanna's story in her voice as she tells the events from her point of view: a luxury she is never given within the biblical account.[2]

I am aware that as I stand within the Christian tradition, I am an outsider and an onlooker to these deep Jewish practices. I have a deep appreciation for the process of writing midrashim. Hence, it is with some tentativeness and with great respect that I seek to open some of the wisdom the Jewish traditions and perspectives offer.

In Judaism, *tikkun olam* means "repairing the world" through social action and spiritual engagements intended to bring about healing of our broken world. Writing a midrash is one of the ways to bring healing into a silence. When we explore the silences in sacred texts, and begin to paint, write poetry, or retell the story, giving voice to the silences, noticing not only the text but also what is behind and beyond the text, we are participating in what is akin to the Jewish tradition of midrash.

When we write a midrash, Rabbi Jill Hammer, author and midrashist, suggests we enter into the scenes and lives of the biblical texts in order to,

> become a character in the action, to wrestle a blessing from the words, to receive a sacred challenge and a powerful gift. We need never fear that we or the Torah will be broken in this mysterious encounter. The text is great enough and strong enough to be profoundly flexible, profoundly generative, even in the modern context where myths are fragile.[3]

So, it was in this spirit of *tikkun olam* that I embarked on the midrash, bringing to this story something of my own experiences of being silenced, while trusting that the text—the living word of God—was strong enough to allow me to "wrestle a blessing from the words."

ENTERING SUSANNA'S SILENCE

The Garden of Eve

If it wasn't so serious it would be funny: reading "Susanna" is like opening the paper one day and reading about your own death in the obituary column. In this case, it does feel a bit like a death. And there is so much that's

---

2. The full text of the book of Susanna is included at the end of this chapter, and the reader may find it helpful to start with reading it through before returning to read the midrash. It is included in Scripture either as chapter 13 in the book of Daniel or placed as a separate book before Daniel.

3. Hammer, *Sisters at Sinai*, xiii–xiv.

not true or not written. Why didn't they just ask me? They all know where to find me, don't they!

And as for the author—what spin! Typical journalist. Who was he? I am not sure, but it is written voyeuristically, inviting all his readers to use their eyes to penetrate my private world! This news article has been titled in one paper as "Susanna's Beauty Attracts Elders," and thus my beauty is to blame! Another has "Seduction by Officials!" But let me tell you, this was a story of abuse and attempted rape.

Anyway. Here's my testimony.

That day when it all began: I remember it well. Come with me on a tour of the garden—that is after all where it all started. Our walled garden was my refuge, my *temenos* I called it fondly: this sanctuary garden, my place of safety and holiness, where I could hear creation breaking bread in the birdsong and the rustling of leaves. Lush, verdant, I liked to think it looked a little like part of the Hanging Gardens. This was my own Garden of Eve, a place to breathe in silence and solitude, away from the busyness of the household after my husband's meetings.

Here I would watch for the small turnings of color on the flesh of the quinces and pomegranates. I always looked out for those telltale bumps on the pomegranates—the prodding, pregnant bumps made by the seeds on the inside telling us that they are getting very juicy and it's almost time to pick. And when it was time for the first one to be plucked, I would invite the family to join me, and our youngest—little Amos—would then symbolically throw the pomegranate down on the clay path to split it open as a celebration and prayer for a fruitful and abundant year. Amid peals of laughter we would all collect pomegranates and greedily suck the juicy seeds, and our cheeks would be plumped red with delight. And the quinces have their own character, their own way of giving thanks to the sun. Hiding their ripeness behind a hard and fragrantless yellow skin with white webbing, they trick me into thinking they will never ripen. Until suddenly, a whole bush will seem to come alive and burst with that unmistakable floral aroma at the last minute, and I plunge my head right into the bush and breathe it all in. Those days I would carry pockets full of quinces and have one in my hand held to my nose as I wandered the garden, immersed in magic scent.

Then there are the herbs and flowers. Pride of place are my now five different types of mint, and the ancient rose stock that gives pungent single-petaled flowers. And of course, lilies—the lines of lilies that speak lyrically of beauty and balance. A garden after all is a poem to be listened to and read, over and over again. Susanna means "lily," a name given to our people, and sometimes refers to young women (so perhaps I will stay forever young). And Susanna is also mentioned by the singer in the Song of Songs (4:12) as representing a sealed garden. (I used to think this was romantic, but it mocks me now.) My sister is called Rakefet, meaning cyclamen, while my two brothers are named after trees: Oren, pine, and Alon, oak. I wonder, does this say something about the hopes of my parents for each of us?

And there are the trees I have watched and nurtured, too. The mastic tree is growing slowly, but I like its shape and it perfumes the air with the smoky-sweet resin smell. I sometimes think it weeps with tears as the resin trickles out, so I have a very soft spot for this sensitive, beautiful tree. We lined the garden wall with date palms; we have one large cedar in the corner and we planted a tamarisk tree right at the center of the garden. Abraham planted a tamarisk in honor of God after the treaty at Beersheba (Gen 21:33), and so we saw it as fitting for this to be our *Nin-Gishzida*, our "trusty tree." It might be an old Mesopotamian myth, but we liked it: the trusty tree can communicate with humans, watches over the garden, guards the gate of heaven, and acts as a law-keeper in the underworld. So we called it *Batach*, Hebrew for trust. I loved sitting under this tree, with its *temenos*-like shady space.

At the center is the now famous pool that used to be a favorite place of mine before all this happened. It is a rectangular shape made out of stone with a small fountain on the side that brings in the spring waters. Small colonnades mark each of the four corners, and I had begun growing a grape vine up the pillars. But I have now stopped tending these. So you can see, this was my sacred space, my *temenos*, my sanctuary—once.

On that day, the day that changed my life, I arose early as usual just before dawn. There was a lot to do, and I preferred to rise before the family, getting a head start on organizing the servants regarding the meals, daily household chores, and preparing for the elders and the holding of court that would fill the house with activity.

I had set aside that morning a long-awaited time to spend with my close friend, Lydia. (Speaking of names, Lydia means "kindred spirit," and indeed she has been.) I have been gifted with a quick mind, so I loved learning the law and am good at applying it. Together with Lydia, we used our times together to develop our own legal frameworks, dreaming of a more emancipated system where women would be equal with men. It kept us sane and with a sense of humor too. You may have noticed from the newspaper article about my story that I was introduced in terms of my relationship with my father Hilkiah (whom I love), and my husband Joakim (whom I adore, and I know he adores me). But I could also have been introduced as the lifelong friend of a kindred spirit, Lydia, the mother of five children, the manager and financial officer of a large household, and a legal researcher and advisor to my husband's decision-making at court.

Joakim knows I have a real handle on the law and a legal mind, so he often discusses the issues brought to court with me, and together we have had a great partnership examining evidence and calling good judgments. We have a respect for each other, which we both cherish. But of course, he can't tell that to a soul—the system is cruel. Even Joakim has been infiltrated by it more than he would like, and I know he wrestles with this. And specks of it lie within me, too; after all, my place in life has been bred into me.

The day was very hot. The previous week had been a heatwave, and the garden was suffering. When at last most of the elders and judges had left our house at the end of the day's debates and judgments, quietness began to descend on our home. None of the elders or judges had any clue about how much I quietly contributed via the ear of my gentle Joakim. His reputation for making wise judgments has grown, and we both joked about how that could possibly happen. We understand each other well. To an extent.

So I was free to wander the garden as I often did at this time of the day. The heat was abating, and I thought it would be an ideal time to swim in the pond, which I have done sometimes with the children. Two of my attendants came with me, and together we watered the wilting plants, speaking words of encouragement to them. I often took this time to speak with Batach. I placed my hand on his trunk. The central trunk was old, grey-brown, and deeply furrowed, and I liked to think I was placing my hand on his aged grandfatherly forehead.

"How are you faring today, with these long hot days we have been having?" I asked him, his needle-like leaves moving softly in the warm wind.

"Tiring," he said, with his sighing voice. "But cooler days will come. And I have my many stems to help me," he said, speaking of some of his smoother, younger trunks growing from his multistemmed base. I leaned against his trunk—sturdy, safe, dependable. His was a safe presence in this garden of mine. On rare occasions I would have a niggle that maybe, just maybe, a serpent from the underworld would make its way into the garden. But then I would shake myself out of such nonsense.

I waited to see if Batach was to say more. But no, just the gentle sighing from him that I had grown to love and to absorb through my skin, like the mint-green of his needles, which seemed to fill the air. The smell I had come to associate with trust and safety. I wandered off to speak with my attendants. As I continued gardening, I had a disturbing sense of a dark, sticky presence. It came close, so quickly, uninvited, oppressive, and began to wrap around me like a dark cloak.

"Who are you?" I demanded to know, as I held my arm out protecting myself from this invisible intruder.

But I already knew who this was. A very familiar enemy that I had long ago named *Totschweigen*, a German word meaning "death by silence." Totschweigen was my internalized voice of complicity with male expectations in this patriarchal society. I knew its power, and I felt unable to quash its persistent silencing of me, like an internal death knell ringing in my ears. Death by silence—a part of me that had come out of my past like a monster emerging from my own murky depths. An old voice, it was always silencing me, telling me I was not worth much, I should keep quiet, not speak as I didn't have anything of value to say, and that I should not expect too much from life. I was to keep my place. And cast my eyes down along with my desires for freedom. But why was he assailing me now?

"Leave!" I commanded, as strongly and convincingly as I could. But it felt hollow, and a defeated heaviness came over me. From childhood my father had a special place for me, but it was a tiny space, a small confined place with no views and no big horizons. I knew this to be my boundary, yet everything within me screamed out that surely there is more. There must be!

"What do you think you are doing out here right now? Shouldn't you be doing something more useful for the household? Isn't there work for Joakim you said you would do for him? Isn't busyness godliness?"

He was sounding like my father, almost reasonable, and very persuasive. Perhaps I shouldn't relax in the pool as I thought I might. I guess I don't deserve to spend more time here. I am just being very selfish.

"See!" Totschweigen exclaimed. "I can tell what you are thinking. I know you well!" I grimaced. He continued in his haranguing voice, "I am right, aren't I! You know I am. You have no right to be out here unless you are working for the household. You know that. Admit it. Joakim can take time out because he works hard." Then he bent forward; his breath smelled foul as he oiled his way around me with his slick slippery skin too close. I could feel myself shaking, as he whispered in that slow, slimy dark voice deep in my ear, "Who do you think you are? Really!"

I swallowed down the burning bile of guilt and embarrassment rising in my throat. What was I thinking? Who did I think I was? I sat down heavily on a rock. I was always told I thought too highly of myself. Even as a child, I was constantly reminded I needed to behave demurely so my father could secure a wealthy husband for me, and so bring honor to the family. I was not to be so rambunctious: silence in a girl is golden, reticence is femininity personified, don't ruffle feathers. My exuberant desire for climbing trees and my secret longing for learning languages, for the law and accounting became a scandal when my mother discovered some of my activities and told my father. I gave in. I traded my soul for my family's honor. But Joakim and I had a certain understanding, didn't we? Joakim. I could picture his gentle face. Oh, how lucky was I to get handed over in marriage to a gentle man, unlike poor Lydia who silently suffered physical beatings from hers. I focused on Joakim—yes, he would say it is fine for me to be spending time here in this place he knows I find so special.

"Joakim understands me! He knows what I do and trusts me, so stop pummelling me with your fists of false words and be banished from here!" I felt a surge of strength coming through me. Joakim did understand me at least a little after all these years we have been together. I would swim today, and defy Totschweigen's quashing, deathlike voice.

I stood up, and tried to push off the oily silence dripping all over me. I stood tall, and began to feel his presence recede. "There we go," I thought to myself. "That's all I had to do. Just stand up to him and shout him down." I felt pleased with myself. I had won, and I could now at least try to remember who I really was, even in this life of limited horizons.

With all the gardening finished, I asked the girls to take some of the produce from the garden to the kitchens, and after that to fetch some minerals for the pool water as it was quite brackish. They were to close and lock the external gates to the garden on their way.

I wandered over to the pool and sat on its edge to wait. I dipped my hands into the cool, earthy-smelling water. I tried to wash my hands of the oily presence of Totschweigen. My skin prickled. "Who do you think you are?" Was it just these words ringing alarm bells, or was it something more sinister I was sensing? I glanced furtively around. Fearful without apparent cause.

Silenced to Death

Out of the corner of my eye, I saw a flicker of movement. Suddenly, from behind the date palms against the wall rushed out two of the elders. I know these people. Yet I see on them unrecognizable faces and piercing eyes. What are they doing here? How did they get in? A flood of questions in that long-frozen moment. Thick blood drummed in my ears. The air turned palely cold.

They seemed to speak at once, gesticulating madly, their arms flinging wide their predatory intentions.

"Look, the garden doors are shut, and no one can see us. We are burning with desire for you; so give your consent, and lie with us! If you refuse," they snarled, "we will testify against you that a young man was with you, and this was why you sent your maids away."

I am trapped! Frozen, held down, and crushed by panic and dread. My garden! My refuge! So much violation!

"Aha! See—you shouldn't have been here at all, being self-indulgent like this. It's all your fault, you know." Totschweigen was coming down heavily on me too. I felt winded and unable to breathe. There was no life left in me. "Your fault, your fault, your fault . . . ." Even my own heartbeat was condemning me.

Everything was starting to turn black, my eyes stung and I could see only a grainy peppered darkness. If I give in to them, the law would have me killed. If I do not, their lie will have me condemned to death. Which death will I choose? Death has closed its hands around my throat. There is nothing left. No one. Only darkness.

Defeated, my back against the wall. I was going to die anyway, so with what little choice I had left, I could decide which death. Oh, cruel fate! I could at least retain my own sense of integrity.

I turned to them, crying out, "I will not!" I could feel a small pulse of energy. "As God sees me now, this is my choice. I refuse to fall into your hands!" And then, rising from a strange deep place inside, came a great primal cry of anger, rage, fear, and defiance that battered against the garden walls and called me up into its surging waves of sound pounding at this prison of pain.

The elders tried to take over the lead in their yelling, and ran to the gate and flung it open. People were running from everywhere, calling out and searching to see what this was all about.

"See! We were in the garden and we caught her in adultery with a young man. He has fled but we caught her red-handed."

I wrapped my arms and robe around me. Stunned, I couldn't move. "You brought this on yourself. How could you do this to your husband? Your family? How could you!" Totschweigen wouldn't give up.

It was then I began to shake, at first just a tremble, and then completely out of control like the day itself, I shook violently. My teeth were chattering, my body ice-cold. The maids who had been on their way to me dropped their jars and ran to my side, holding me up. I leaned on them heavily as they helped me from the garden, and we made our way through the silent crowd. Not a sound. A deathly silence. No words of comfort. No understanding glances. Even our faithful household servants were looking so ashamed of me.

I don't remember much about what happened after that. I know Joakim came in and stood for a long while at the door of my room. I couldn't raise my eyes. For a moment I thought he might come, sit beside me, and ask what really happened. Say something like, "This is not the Susanna I know," and I would be comforted by his knowledge of who I really am and I would have a safe place to tell him what really happened. And he would believe me. But instead I felt him turn to leave. I raised my eyes just enough to see his back as he made his way down the hall, a little unsteady on his feet. I leaned back into the dark emptiness of the night.

After what felt like hours of numb disbelief, I fell into a fitful sleep, waking on and off to the crooning-groaning sound of the wind outside, with visions of the mastic tree weeping for me, and Batach, a grounded guardian unable to protect me after all. Exhaustion overtook me, and I slept then until woken by my two maids.

I could hear the elders and judges beginning to gather for the court session. Joakim came and told me it was time for me to come before them and hear their judgment. His face was deeply lined, pained, but told me nothing. I followed him into the room, and I was guided to stand before them. I glanced around. All eyes were on me. And there were the two—the two evil elders staring, glaring at me. They looked so vicious with their wolf-like faces, baring their teeth and salivating with victory. I couldn't breathe. I focused on my feet, hoping they would hold me steady. I knew my parents and children were gathered there too, but I could not bear to look at them. I felt so alone, so abandoned; a vacuum had opened out and there was no one, no God, no help, nothing.

"Take off her veil!" It was one of the elders. I froze. Someone came and took off my veil, leaving me exposed, humiliated to the core. I felt eyes penetrating my soul, violating every inch of my being. That penetrating look was so defiling! I could see my family weeping—with me? Or for me? Who did they believe? And there were all the *onlookers* (so much captured by one word!).

As the two elders approached, the same evil stench of presence sent shock waves through me as it triggered the stench of yesterday. Then the most egregious thing happened. They placed their greedy, damning hands on my head, in my hair. This, apparently, was their "right"! I retched and my legs went to jelly, but I did not—would not—give in. I could hear my children whimpering.

My body gave way to tears I couldn't control, as if my soul was trying to flush out this defilement. I lifted my head up, pushing against their heavy hands and looked deeply into heaven, wishing myself out of this world. I would all too soon be in my eternal home. I tried to breathe and calm myself.

The two then began their speech: "As we were walking in the garden alone, this woman came in with her maids, shut the garden doors, and dismissed the maids. Then a young man, who had been hidden, came to her and lay with her. We were in a corner of the garden, and when we saw this wickedness, we ran to them. We saw them embracing, but we could not hold the man, for he was too strong for us, and he opened the doors and dashed out. So we seized this woman and asked her who the young man was, but she would not tell us. These things we testify."

A commotion of condemnation followed. No one was asking me to speak of my version of events. No one gave thought to me to be able to defend myself. I had been silenced by the elders, by Totschweigen, by the judges, by the crowds who assumed knowledge of the truth. I was condemned to death. What they didn't know was that I had already died. I had nothing left and nothing to lose. I released my soul and felt its winged softness lift away like the moth's last flight into the sun. I cried out my final death song, lifting my voice with all the strength I had left so that every corner in heaven would reverberate with my cry: "Everlasting God, you know all secrets, and are aware of all things before they come to be. You know that they have given false evidence against me. And now I am to die, though I have done none of the wicked things that they have falsely charged against me."

There was silence. A brittle silence—nothing from heaven, nothing from ashen Joakim standing stung and stunned, nothing from my parents who knew me from birth. Yet despite everything, I knew somehow that God was God, and heaven would be a reprieve. There I would find a real garden of Eden where I would never again be violated, an everlasting *temenos* where no evil could penetrate. Terror mixed with a small slice of relief. Two judges then led me out into the harsh sunlight and into the heat of the crowd outside.

An Emerging Story

Suddenly I became aware of a different voice above the crowd's, and there was a buzz of confusion as a man I later heard was called Daniel pushed through to the front of the crowd. He shouted out loudly, "I am innocent of the blood of this woman." Those that were leading me increased their grip on my arm as we all turned to see who this was and what was happening.

"Are you such fools, you sons of Israel? Have you condemned a daughter of Israel without examination and without learning the facts? Return to the place of judgment. For these men have borne false witness against her."

Who was this young man? What was motivating him to speak on my behalf? Had God indeed been aroused and awakened him to my plight? I was beyond trusting any man now. I felt numb as I was led back into what had been my own home, for another session of court. Heaven still felt so much better than this continued mockery of justice. When would it end? I felt stronger now, as if being reconciled to death gave me a clarity I hadn't been able to access until now.

The crowd seemed to have swelled, but my grounded stance helped me to block out all the eyes that kept doing strip searches of me. I stared back defiantly, my eyes able to be steadier and truer than theirs. I could feel my dignity straightening my spine and lifting my head and I felt tall and strong. I was who I was, and no one could take that away, regardless of what might befall me.

An elder who had said little during the proceedings so far gave Daniel permission to speak. "Separate these two who bring these testimonies, and I will examine them separately before you." Daniel sounded older than his years, and had a confidence about him.

When the one elder stood before him out of earshot of his accomplice, Daniel raised his voice. "You old relic of wicked days, your sins have now come home, which you have committed in the past, pronouncing unjust judgments, condemning the innocent and letting the guilty go free, though the LORD said, 'Do not put to death an innocent and righteous person.'" There were murmurs among the crowd. How did Daniel know this elder? And what wickedness was there in this elder's past? How then, had he been made an elder and judge?

"Now then," Daniel continued when people had quietened down, "if you really saw her, tell me this: under what tree did you see them being intimate with each other?"

He answered, "Under a mastic tree." Oh, my heart! My beloved weeping tree.

Daniel replied, "Very well! You have lied against your own head, for the angel of God has received the sentence from God." There were gasps in the crowd. The angel of God! This meant God was intervening—God had heard my cry. Dare I believe it? But I had to wait, things were still not clear. I looked across at Joakim, and realized he had been watching me with gentle eyes, as if he had known all along and yet . . . what had he done to exercise his power? Why did he not . . . No, I couldn't go there right now. This whole cultural system of ours has not only cut my wings, but trapped so many good men as well. Was Daniel breaking free? He continued, "Because you chose the mastic tree, the tree that bleeds its life sap when cut, you will now be condemned to be cut in two, spilling out your own lifeblood."

The elder's face went white, and he was taken and held at the back of the crowd. I watched as the other was led in. Again, Daniel addressed him with such surety, "You offspring of Canaan and not of Judah, beauty has deceived you and lust has perverted your heart."

My heart sank. Was this still condemning me—stating it was *my* beauty that could actively "deceive" another? How could I have caused this lust? Daniel continued, "This is how you both have been dealing with the daughters of Israel, and they were intimate with you through fear; but a daughter of Judah would not endure your wickedness." Had this man done so much more damage to many already? How was this not known before? Why had this man been made an elder and judge of others? Why had the community been silent on this and not already brought them both to trial? So many questions, and so many heartbreaking revelations. Here at last truth was breaking though.

"Now then, tell me: under what tree did you catch them being intimate with each other?" The elder answered, "Under an evergreen oak." I don't even have one of those in the garden! How delusionary. Daniel said to him, "Very well! You also have lied against your own head, for the angel of God is waiting with his sword to saw you in two, that you may be forever destroyed."

There was an eruption of shouting and acclamation. I could hardly let myself trust what was happening. "Oh God," I sighed deeply, "You have truly heard my cry and brought your angels to intervene, to judge rightly. I have been heard at last, and this by you, the Eternal One of the Universe no less." I knew from my own knowledge of the law that the elders were condemned by their own hand. These false witnesses had now brought upon their own heads the punishment they had planned for me.

I turned to Totschweigen who was hovering disturbingly at my shoulder. "Well?" I said, looking him straight in the eye. "You nearly had your way, but you didn't succeed!" He continued hovering in that menacing way; then he simply scoffed, smiled darkly, and faded into the shadows of the crowd. I knew he would be back.

But I also knew that, in my cry to God against all the odds, I could recognize my true strong self emerging again. It would take me a long time to go back to that defiled garden. But I knew I could survive. Within my own self was a monastic garden of the most exquisite kind where the loving Spirit danced with my spirit. (I will take you on a tour one day when we have time.)

I was standing in the noisy crowd, and now for the first time it seemed I was invisible. People around me were praising God, thanking God "for saving those who hope in God alone." People were hugging and patting each other on the back saying, "Justice has been seen this day," and "God has spoken." Interesting, I thought, how suddenly things have reversed, and I am now almost ignored, invisible as they congratulate one another around me. I felt a sudden thump against my legs and it was Amos, our five-year-old, wrapping his arms around me, sobbing and laughing at the same time. I scooped him up in my arms, and looked around. I could see my father and mother in praise of God lifting their arms and eyes to heaven. The household honor had been upheld.

Joakim broke away from the rest of the family where he too had been praising God, and made his way over to me. I knew Joakim was still trapped in this power-paradigm. He was stunned, paralyzed. Unable to respond, defend, or even question. But that's the power of the system, isn't it? We stood in silence together. Nothing would be the same again. A long journey lay ahead of us.

And so, those lecherous preying elders were put to death in my place. I didn't leap for joy. The structures haven't changed. It will be repeated again by others tomorrow, and there may not be a Daniel around then. And Daniel, dear Daniel was hailed as the hero that day. Well, I am beyond heroizing, which comes and goes like a flash in the pan. But integrity and truth: I thirst for them. And I know deep within me that my life is bedded with truth, which cuts between bone and marrow—dynamic, strong, vibrant, shining—and lasts beyond all fleeting acclamations.

Now, I have told my story. I hope I have helped repair the great gaping wound caused by the oppression of silence and the onslaught of untruths. Perhaps it will help you with your own story, or someone else's.

But I will not forget what has happened. So, I close with a litany before my God of the multiple invasions and violations by those who:

> abused their power and desecrated my home with their evil intent and disregard for truth;
> invaded my privacy of self by their deliberate looking with perverted intent;
> violated my husband and my hospitality and our relationship;
> trespassed into my precious garden, breaking through boundaries with rape in mind to physically penetrate me.

They then
> polluted my integrity by telling untruths about me,
> invaded my sense of self by demanding I "unveil" publicly and then molested my personhood, laying their hands on my head as if I were a sacrifice to be offered.

But there is more:
> I stand clear as having no guilt whatsoever.
> I claimed myself with my integrity in the face of overwhelming evil.
> I called out and voiced my need to the Truthing God who hears me

And the Just One answered,
> The Risen One descended into my hell, pulling me free
> Praise be to God!

REFLECTION

Gifts from the World of Midrash

I first read the book of Susanna while doing some theological studies, and was immediately drawn into her story, finding myself irresistibly curious about her situation. It seemed to me her predicament resonated down through the centuries still, and struck a chord in my own heart. After some background reading, I wanted to get to know Susanna, to touch her life and let her life touch mine. The possibility of using a midrash to do that opened a wondrous door into the world of Jewish exegesis and textual interpretation. *Tikkun olam*—the healing of Susanna, of myself, indeed of all Susannas—became my motivating desire as I ventured into Susanna's garden.

Writing with the voice of Susanna allowed some of my own experience to join with hers, and together it seemed we were able to give voice to the unvoiced wounds as well as the possibilities, empowering us to write our own endings to our stories and sing together a litany of truth. In this way, the book of Susanna became for me a resistance text, and midrash the vehicle offering both protest and freedom.

Unlike the hermeneutical guidelines I have grown up with in the Christian tradition, midrash seemed to give me wings. No longer was I approaching the text with fear and trembling, lest I misread or misinterpret it, and get it "wrong." Rather, I was given permission by the tradition of midrash to travel as an explorer into the infinite depth of meaning and possible lessons, knowing that the text is robust and revelatory for all time periods and all cultures, all situations, and all peoples.

Midrash lies in the midst of the Jewish interpretive practice called *pardes* (PRDS)[4] as a way to delve into the *Tanakh* (Hebrew Scriptures). This is a fourfold approach.[5] The P represents *peshat*, and is the literal or surface meaning. The R refers to *remez*, which is the more allegorical or symbolic meaning. *Derash* is the D, the metaphorical meaning, including word associations, engaging the active imagination. This is where midrash (*darash*, meaning "to inquire, seek") takes place. The last layer, S or the *sod*, is the discovery of a hidden meaning or mystical applications.

---

4. Frankel, *Sacred Therapy*, 3; Stein, *Introduction to the Parables of Jesus*, 47.

5. In an email discussion with Rabbi Addison, I was alerted to the fact that this fourfold mode of exegesis was found in the writings of the Venerable Bede of the eighth century, and probably served as a model for what was then adopted by Baḥya ben Asher of Saragossa (1291), who then went on to make this a popular exegetic method with the *Tanakh*.

As it turns out, *pardes* also means "orchard." As I took time to reflect on Susanna, it was as if I was wandering through the orchard—but in this orchard, the trees were the verses. Strolling through the trees, I began at first to view the landscape at the more superficial level. A sacred text. A story. With a victim, a false accusation, a prayer and the last-minute intervention of a hero. Then I began to notice further nuances, the *remez*, such as the violation of not only Susanna but also of her sacred spaces. "Beauty" was held up throughout as the cause of the whole debacle, with the blame resting on Susanna right to the end. The responsiveness of Daniel to God's prompting and his astuteness. This now led me down the avenue of *derash*, embarking on a midrash and reimagining the story from Susanna's viewpoint and mine. The *sod*—unfolding the mystical or hidden meaning—is something that is ongoing, continuing through the seeds of the orchard's fruit. So, when we wander through an orchard such as *pardes*, we can simply notice the fruit on the tree, take the time to admire it, and leave it there. Or we can go further and pluck, wash, peal, and slice it. Going deeper into *daresh* means we eat the fruit, savor its taste and texture, swallow it, and it feeds us. And the mystical meaning then emerges: we become what we eat.

And as I explored the orchard of the book of Susanna, and embodied her voice and experience, I encountered again the questioning of what God's withholding from early and speedy intervention is about. It is one of the recurring experiences I have, when God seems to be absent, silent, and choosing as it were deliberately not to step in and protect, or bring justice. I know that it is impossible theoretically for God to be absent if God is indeed God. In writing the midrash, I was aware that in the original text God did indeed intervene, but what was the delay for? And for me it raised again my deep human yearning and tension that this ever-present God demonstrate attentiveness by breaking into history and bring goodness out of evil, destruction, and violence before too much damage is done. In Susanna, I embodied my own past experience, and I couldn't let the opportunity pass without exploring her desperation at this "delaying God."

Since I was in this world of Jewish wisdom, I journeyed deeper into Jewish mysticism to find some clue, some solace. Here I came across the Kabbalistic-Hasidic concept of *tzimtzum* (Hebrew: contraction/constriction). It refers to the Kabbalistic interpretation of the Genesis story, which sees God's choosing to contract God's self (including infinite light) to make space for creation of the finite world.[6]

It is important to note that ontologically it is not possible for God actually to be absent, but rather God has contracted God's self at an energetic

6. Rotenberg, *Psychology of Tzimtzum*, 6–7.

level, since the created world is unable to withstand the force of divine energy. Consequently, the commonly suggested idea of "making space," which implies complete absence, is not accurate. God is still present via the Shechinah, and is immanent in God's creation, but *we* experience this as absence owing to its perceived evanescence.

This contraction can result in finite humanity struggling with the *sense* of the absence of God. Yet the space created through *tzimtzum*, I discovered, is seen as profoundly hospitable, opening a space in order for humanity to have a home. A metaphor that helped me here is the life-saving ring used at sea. The ring has a hole enabling space for me, yet the hole does not exist independently of the ring, and it is the open hole that enables saving action. Anyone who finds themselves in such a hole knows its depth of angst and the life-threatening experience it is. One is incapable of retrieving oneself from such a situation; all one can do is hang on desperately to the ring. And so according to *tzimtzum*, there is a deep union of the whole in the paradox of simultaneous presence and absence. This helped me as I continued not only with Susanna but also with my own dark holes. God is indeed the God who is there, and who comes . . . in God's own way and time.

As I leaned into the ring to hold on as I wrote, so Susanna leaned against the sturdy trunk of Batach. She later leans onto her maids to get help to leave the garden, and then in the loneliness of the night she leans into "the dark emptiness of the night." Her leaning into the empty darkness was a leaning back into the *perceived* absence of God. We know rationally it is not possible for God to become absent to any of God's creation, yet the experience of abandonment is no less a deathlike experience. Jesus experienced a godforsakenness on the cross. When we cry out to God and sense no response at all, could it be that this cry is God's cry in us; our longing for connection is God's own longing within is, and our desire to reach God is God's desire to reach us? Is this the infilling of the *tzimtzum* hole?

The Multiple Violations

As I wrote the midrash, one of the realizations for me was the way multiple layers of violation kept on being uncovered. First, there was Susanna's walled garden. That glorious space that she had loved and nurtured was her *temenos*. But what was meant to protect her became that which was used to condemn her. Then of course the violation of her own sense of safety, her soul, her dignity, and her sense of self. As I wrote about Totschweigen, I was reminded how words that condemn and diminish said by an abuser can so violate personal inner space that we take on such a voice as our own.

This voice of inflicting silence, and insisting everything is my fault, and I am to blame persists in the story right to the end, because although much dimmed now, it continues to be one of my inner voices, and it knows my weak points. So it was very healing for me that Susanna allowed me to name and portray this dark presence, to externalize it, to have it defeated at the end, but also to acknowledge that "I knew he would be back." Because indeed I know he will be.

Other violations include those that affect relationships: her reputation has been damaged, probably irreparably; the relationship between Susanna and Joakim has been deeply cracked; her children have experienced the trauma of watching their mother and their sense of security must have been undermined, and their home has now become a place of accusation and terrifying memories. In embodying Susanna's damaged relationships, I became grateful, realizing how much I have been learning in the wisdom of how to manage broken relationships that have a very long tail, hopeful that hers too would slowly find a place to sit within her life story in a way that would bring empowerment.

I cringed when I wrote about the elders placing their hands on Susanna's head. Usually such a gesture is part of a blessing in the Hebrew Scriptures—a wondrous and beautiful touch. But here, just as sacrificial animals have hands laid on their heads, the elders are sacrificing Susanna for their own ends. This indeed is a touch that violates. Many of us experience such touches—touches that seek not to give in affirmation but to take what is not being offered, and they need not be gender-based. So it was a sobering exercise for me to trace all these threads of violation, and how they reflected parts of my own experience.

Gendered Viewing

When exploring a narrative, it can be illuminating to bear three questions in mind: Who acts? Who sees? Who speaks?[7] Acting, speaking, but also seeing can violate. The way of seeing engaged in by the two elders who embodied evil, "penetrated" and "defiled" Susanna's privacy.[8] The repetitive use of the words "see," "look," and associated words such as "onlookers" used by Theodotian (writer of the biblical account), invite us to become aware of the powerful impact eyes can have. And this includes all forms of gendered viewing beyond just male and female, which tear down rather than affirm another.

7. Bal, *Anti-Covenant*, 17.
8. Jordan and Chang, "Penetration of Private Places," 3.

Being in Susanna's skin, as it were, enabled me to notice my own bodily reactions as I attempted to release Susanna's voice into freedom. I noticed how I my stomach churned and I struggled to find what I thought needed to be the chinks in the narrator's way of seeing and telling the story. I felt tense, restricted, and frustrated. It took quite a while before I realized that, together with Susanna, we were not needing to look for tiny slices of space to voice our part, but rather we had the freedom to simply create not only a new storyteller's voice, but a whole new story. I found it liberating when Susanna flouted conventions and broke silence, crying out her "death song" to God. When shame would normally mean her eyes should have been cast down, she defied expectations and turned her eyes to heaven—the place that the elders found so difficult to focus upon—and thus threw off the cloak of oppression and prayed a courageous and valiant prayer. In a very real way, we might say Susanna had this strength because she had accepted her death already. She had died before she had died as it were, crucified with Christ, and it was no longer she that lived but Christ within her (Gal 2:20).

Beyond Heroizing

According to the biblical version, God responded to Susanna's prayer, aroused the spirit of Daniel, and gave him a wisdom and authority beyond his years to call things to a halt. The silence from God that Susanna had experienced was turned into action by God's Spirit, and angels began to get involved. The silencing of her voice put her at the mercy of others. Here Daniel acted as an ally, raised up by God. The fact that he did not speak up earlier would seem to suggest he did not have this insight then. It is only after Susanna's prayer that he is prompted to act and given wisdom with the judgments coming from angels.

Susanna's prayer could be held up as an example of robust resistance in the midst of evil oppression. Some may feel her response weak, bowing to the male cultural mores. But for me, this was a powerful recognition that we cannot bring about revolution on our own, and that God alone is Creator and the Supreme Judge of all. Her strength of character in her context shines through this prayer of surrender into the hands of God alone—trustworthy hands. And as with Daniel (and my own inner voice of Totschweigen), God can break us all free from being complicit with injustice. Such a movement of God can be hopeful. If we can rest in the knowledge that God *is* God, and *is* good, and *is* always, always present to us in all circumstances, then we can begin to know that justice and truth will indeed reign, if not now, then in and for eternity.

If there needs to be a hero or a focal point, it rightly lies with Susanna and her relationship with God. As I wrote this midrash, I was again struck by the dignity that she retained throughout the proceedings, as well as her deep Job-like stance with God, "See, he will kill me; I have no hope; but I will defend my ways to his face" (Job 13:15). This is the mystery that breaks in through the Easter Holy Saturday descent of Christ into hell with us, and is the love of God in Christ "reaching to heal, to soothe, to save—even and especially there, when I am free-falling to a bottom that knows no bottom. For God's love is without measure, beyond calculation. It knows no bounds."[9]

In the end, in the biblical version, Daniel is lauded and God is praised for saving those who hope in God. Susanna drops out of the scene completely. She is the pretext for the ascendency of Daniel, which could look like the reward of God resting upon him as his reputation grows as a result of his obeying God. And Susanna? In my midrash account I felt it was important for her to rise above needing to be acclaimed or praised. That the deeper and more lasting affirmation was her own profound courage in finding and using her true voice with God in what was a desperately difficult situation. She illustrated that women's dignity and ascendency did not depend on male recognition, but were rather within her own gift, with the help of God. Some may disagree with me here, in that we do not see rightful acclamation of Susanna, or changed structures in society as a result of what happened; even so, perhaps the fact that we are reading about her now shows that justice does come, but not necessarily in our timeframes.

Susanna Continues as a Resistance Text

Susanna's voice continues to reverberate down through the centuries and into our laps. One powerful element of resistance is found with all survivors: the ultimate resistance is to survive, to become truly alive and claim their space anew. Susanna encourages me with her strength, independence, and wisdom. And so when I wrote the litany at the end of the story, it felt as if I was joining with all people who have suffered any abuse of power, and this time it was a bursting-out of a liberation song, a healing song in the service of *tikkun olam*, a song of truth-telling and life shouted from the rooftops.

There is silence regarding what happens to Susanna after all this is over. Yet we can know that the silence of God is a productive and eternal silence, one in which God sees with soft eyes of eternal love and compassion, with

9. Downey, *Depth of God's Reach*, ch. 9, section: "Luminous Traces in the Dark," para. 7.

the eyes of one who birthed us into the world; a Trinitarian God who never takes their eyes off their children. We will continue to see the unfolding fecundity of this story. Like pomegranate seeds, there will be a profusion of joy and abundant scatterings that bring fruit in due season as more and more people sit in the garden with Susanna, and listen as she tells her story.

PONDERING YOUR OWN EXPERIENCES

- You may wish to write your own midrash, focusing on Susanna, Joakim, Daniel, or one of the maids as way of entering deeply into Scripture, and being open to receiving a blessing, challenge, and gift, and thus participating in repairing the world.

- "This was my sacred space, my *temenos*, my sanctuary—once." What are your *temenos* spaces? You may wish to reflect on times during your life when you found yourself in places meant for protection, but in fact became places where you felt trapped. If you have lost what was once a sacred and safe place for you, what new place can you find? And how can you become the embodiment of *temenos* in such a way that your presence can provide safe spaces for others?

- "I had been silenced by the elders, by Totschweigen, by the judges, by the crowds who assumed knowledge of the truth." When have you or someone you are close to been silenced? How did this occur? Was there within yourself an internal push for silence (this could have been from a healthy or not-so-healthy voice)? What can you learn from this experience? Is there a way this equips you to help others to find their voice? You may wish to notice if there are any ways in which you have become complicit with structural injustice and if there is some change you can initiate.

- "What they didn't know was that I had already died. I had nothing left and nothing to lose." Susanna's prayer is also her testimony. Are there some movements towards healthy nonattachment that you want to take? What prayers have sustained you? And what prayers have you written that give you voice?

- "I am beyond heroizing, which comes and goes like a flash in the pan. But integrity and truth: I thirst for them. And I know deep within me that my life is bedded with truth, which cuts between bone and marrow—dynamic, strong, vibrant, shining—and lasts beyond all fleeting acclamations." What is your deep desire now?

FOR FURTHER ENGAGEMENT

Midrash: Voicing the Silenced

The word midrash (midrashim, plural) is a Hebrew word meaning "to search out, to seek, to inquire."[10] According to Curzon, midrashim tend to have three basic elements: they are responses to a specific text, they are imaginative, and they aim to make a point. A midrash is based on the assumption that Scripture holds infinite depth of meaning and lessons for us; it is a text that is open-ended. As such, one of the hermeneutical assumptions of the midrash is that current issues and frameworks can be brought to bear on ancient texts, since the texts are robust and revelatory for all time periods and all cultures. Midrashim, therefore, may take many forms. Any poetry based on the biblical text may be seen as a form of midrash.[11] It is a creative way of engaging the text, and in many ways the retelling of the biblical story by many preachers can be said to be a type of midrash.

There is a growing movement called the Network of Biblical Storytellers, whose members memorize Scripture in order to retell it with reference to the original oral tradition. In the retelling, the way silences are inserted and with what impact, as well as emphases chosen, all serve to interpret the text and thus become a more subtle form of midrash. Paintings, songs, music, drama, and dialogue may all take the form of a midrash if they seek to discover meaning, interpretation, and application. Theopoetics also offers creative responses to texts, where the lived or embodied experience of a text is honored along with aesthetic and poetic responses. It enables departure from a rigid hermeneutic to artistic meaning-making.[12] In both midrash and theopoetics we see the role of imagination at the service of transformative creativity.

As we write a midrash, seeking to open Scripture and giving a place for the living word of God to come to us again in new ways, releasing silenced voices, hidden truths, and transfiguring encounters, it becomes a contribution to repairing the world. This imperative of Judaism, to contribute to the healing of the world (*tikkun olam*), reminds us not only to avail ourselves of healing and repair, but that taking a role in healing our environment, even by small incremental choices, is the essence of *tikkun olam*.

In desiring to contribute to a better world, writing a midrash can be done as prayer, in dialogue with God, sanctifying our imagination, and can even be a form of worship. It is a way of getting to know the characters in a

10. Curzon, *Modern Poems on the Bible*, 4.

11. Curzon, *Modern Poems on the Bible*, 20.

12. See, e.g., Keefe-Perry, *Way to Water*.

text, honoring their place in history and what they have done, and retelling the story again today, bringing their voices and gifts into our context as a dialogue, polemic, challenge, or inspiration, calling us to a deeper knitting together into the God Who Cares. It can also be done in a mystical other-worldly sense, much like imaginative fiction. For example, in one beautiful and mystical midrash from the Zohar on Israel's crossing of the sea, it is said that the Song at the Sea was "sung by embryos in the womb."[13] This evoca-tive phrase beckons our imaginations to picture what kind of experience this might have been for all the pregnant women who were crossing from Egypt into the new land, wondering what would lie ahead for their yet un-born children. It evokes the way babies kick when they hear a familiar voice, or for Christians it touches on Elizabeth's experience of John leaping within her womb at the sound of Mary's arrival at her door. It is a particularly lovely touch of the way supernatural wonder in a story can communicate important messages.

One of the main motivations for Hammer, as a midrashist, is to "fill in the white spaces" within the texts; the vast realm of interpretation of these spaces is "already hidden in the Torah, and it is up to us to find it."[14] And she goes on to sum up her experience by suggesting: "Midrash is an act of repairing the world, because it seeks to uncover the voices that the text does not hold and forces us to listen to what these voices say."[15] Liberating silenced voices is one of the gifts midrashim can give to the world.

The Book of Susanna and the Silence of God

There are a few versions of the Susanna story. That which is included at the end of this chapter forms part of the Apocrypha and is included in the Revised Standard Version Catholic edition of the Bible as Daniel 13. This is commonly referred to as the Theodotian version; sixty-four verses, assumed to be written around the second century CE but set in the Babylonian exile during the Persian period 500 BCE. The book of Susanna is excluded from the Hebrew *Tanakh* and in contemporary Protestant canons of Scripture, but included in Catholic, Orthodox, and Amish canons.

Interestingly, even though it is set in the time of the exile, Susanna's household is obviously wealthy and does not give the impression of a cul-ture in lament by the waters of Babylon. Despite her wealth and the relative

---

13. Hammer, *Sisters at Sinai*, section: "The Bones of Joseph," para. 5.

14. Hammer, *Sisters of Sinai*, section: Introduction, para. 2.

15. Hammer, *Sisters of Sinai*, section: "The Tree with Roots and Wings: Sources of Midrash," para. 6.

power of her husband, she is still not protected from violence. "Representing the threatened covenant community, she is already a warning to those who would enjoy social privileges in foreign settings: no garden is safe."[16] Some critics suggest that Susanna (meaning "lily," which is used in other texts to refer to the Jewish nation) does not just represent one woman, but is also a metaphor for Israel in exile surrounded by enemies, with the elders representing the predatory evil power of Babylon. But unlike Israel, Susanna escapes their power.

One haunting element for those in deep suffering is the experience of the silence of God. In a short space such as this, there are only a few small things to be offered regarding such an excruciatingly painful mystery. Werner Jeanrond, a German Catholic theologian with interests in the theologies of love and hope, expresses it well: "God's silence is not always a welcome silence, since often we wish God to speak, to denounce injustice, to say what we wish to hear, and to legitimate what we wish to do. God's silence is disconcerting, troubling, and disruptive of our plans, hopes, and schemes. God's silence remains a terrible challenge for us."[17] The omnipotent, omniscient all-loving God becoming apparently absent to us remains a disconcerting paradox, especially when we are in extremis. Jeanrond refers to an experience of Elie Wiesel, a survivor of Auschwitz, where he could not see God's presence in any beauty, but he could see the painful image of God in the corpse of a hanging child in the gallows.[18]

There are times when each of us may be called to be the mouthpieces of God, speaking out the silent spaces through midrash, art, poetry, liturgy, and ritual or music. In this way we embody the presence of God. Martin Laird, writing on Christian contemplative spirituality, describes a ritual in the Catholic tradition where, during the Holy Saturday vigil, a cross is carved into a candle and, in the five locations where Jesus was wounded—head, both hands, side, and feet—is placed a seed of fragrant incense. Laird describes how this "theology in wax" speaks great wisdom: "Because of the death and resurrection of Jesus, all wounds, failure, disgrace, death itself all have the hidden potential for revealing our deepest ground in God. Our wounds bear the perfumed trace of divine perspective."[19] Simply meditating on such powerful symbolism touches deeply, and grasps us in ways a series of propositional statements describing the theology cannot. It is indeed a

---

16. Levine, "Hemmed in on Every Side," 312.

17. Jeanrond, "Love and Silence," 17.

18. Jeanrond, "Love and Silence," 17.

19. Laird, *Into the Silent Land*, 120.

form of midrash in wax, releasing a wisdom that can apprehend us in transfiguring ways.

Along with Susanna, we have other people of great wisdom to whom we can refer, who also have undergone such deep wounding from being silenced. Rabia of Basra (717–801), was born into a family of deep poverty in a small town in Iraq. At a young age she was orphaned, and sold into slavery. There is some controversy surrounding exactly what kind of life she had, but Ladinsky,[20] among others, has suggested that the slavery included abuse and being forced to work in a brothel. Considering she was not released into freedom until she was in her fifties, this indicates a sustained time of great suffering. Yet once freed, she became revered for her wisdom and godliness, was sought out for guidance, and is now known as one of the most influential Sufi mystics. Forged from her own experience, one of the poems attributed to her speaks of her elevation and experience of true Love and how such Love's stillness is far from passive. She writes, "Love is / the perfect stillness / and the greatest excitement, and the most profound act / and the word almost as complete / as His name."[21]

And too, the psalmists' voices come down through the ages, wrapping words around the wounds of silence. In Psalm 42, the psalmist despairs, as people goad him because they can see the excruciating experience of the absence of God in the psalmist's life. "My only food day and night are my tears; they recriminate me: 'Where is your God?' they say. . . . I say to God my rock, 'Why have you forgotten me? Why do you keep me in mourning, oppressed by an unseen enemy?' My bones are shattered by their words, foes taunt me constantly, 'Where is your God?' they say" (Ps 42: 3, 9–10).[22] Peppered through the psalm is an attempt to bring in hope, to encourage the soul. We also know that it was in the silence, aloneness, and darkness of the tomb where Jesus lay that the resurrection happened. Resurrections happen in such places. Yet there is no attempt here at all to justify suffering of any kind, nor to give the book of pain a nice cover. It is what it is: profound, unspeakable torment and decimation. Writing on Jewish narratives of journey, Jewish author and spiritual director, Barbara Breitman, like the psalmist, speaks to our souls:

> Loss and suffering can be powerful engines of spiritual growth precisely because grief destroys the ego's illusions of autonomy, dominance, and control. Those who are able to let an older version of self die, so a newly enlarged sense of self can emerge,

20. Ladinsky, *Love Poems from God*.
21. Ladinsky, *Love Poems from God*, 5.
22. Priests for Equality, *Inclusive Bible*.

undergo a profound transformation. . . . When the heart breaks open, it can encompass more of the world within it, and a person can discover new meaning and purpose through serving a larger circle of life.[23]

Reading Susanna Today: Gendered Viewing

If we notice who sees, who speaks, and who acts in the story of Susanna, it is clear that we are being told the story through patriarchal eyes, reducing her to a silenced object. Glancy points out that masculinity is associated with subject-status and femininity with object-status, with the concept of "gaze" so often being associated with man as the subject of the gaze, and woman as the object. She goes on to say, "To see is to control; to have one's vision represented is to have one's perception of the world ratified. To be seen is to be subject to control; to represent women solely as objects of others' vision denies women their subjectivity."[24]

And there is a need to be aware of the damage that can be done when a binary understanding of gender allows for only male or female lenses for viewing. Much biblical scholarship has ignored the implications of the frequent use of merism in Scripture. Merism is a figure of speech which describes an extended concept by referring to only two (often opposing) elements of the whole. For example, when we read in Genesis 1:1 that God created "the heavens and the earth," the phrase is describing the whole universe. Similarly, in Genesis 1:5 the creation by God of evening and of morning is suggestive of the whole day—all that lies in between. In creating light and darkness, again, God is creating these as well as all the shades of light and dark in between. When the psalmist in Psalm 139:2 speaks of God: "You know when I sit down and when I rise up," we automatically understand that this means all of one's activities. In the same way, then, when Genesis 1:27 says, "Humankind was created as God's reflection: in the divine image God created them; female and male, God made them,"[25] this too needs to be seen with the consistency with which the other verses have been understood: that this is a merism, and therefore refers to male and female and all that is in between. We need to view one another with soft eyes that affirm each person as created in the image of God.

---

23. Breitman, "Spiritual Transformations," section: "Deeper into the Wilderness," para. 6.

24. Glancy, "Accused: Susanna and Her Readers," 105.

25. Priests for Equality, *Inclusive Bible.*

The narrator's view of Susanna as a seductress and tempter has been perpetuated by a profusion of art responses over the centuries. Such painterly presentations continue to draw the viewer into a voyeuristic seeing of the scene, thus joining the elders and narrator in making the continual viewing of Susanna as an object. With reference to narrative strategies, Old Testament scholar Cheryl Exum has poignantly coined the phrase "raped by the pen."[26] In Susanna's case, one might be justified in saying she has been raped by both pen and paint. I could find very little art that depicts Susanna as strong, or vocalizing her prayer in the midst of the court, even though this is the pivotal point in the whole story, the point of greatest power and impact. I found one woodcut from 1860 that portrays the trial of Susanna. She is standing to one side with her hands clasped in prayer. It depicts Susanna as devout and demure, but to my mind fails to portray her as a woman of agency and strength who could exercise trust and faith in God in the midst of extreme pressure and threat of death. It was Susanna and her courageous, outrageous prayer and the subsequent act of God that provide the heroic foci in the story. Yet it is Daniel in the end who is cited as the hero, the one who saves Susanna—not Susanna's own voice and prayer, which God hears and responds to so powerfully. The continuation of disbelief in Susanna's complete innocence reflects current experiences of those who speak out about abuse and gender violence. That continued disbelief perpetuates the abuse.

The separating of the two elders has an important message as another element of violence against Susanna emerges in the form of male solidarity against her. The two elders support one another in their desire to rape Susanna, and then their high position in society bonds them with the other male judges to act in solidarity against her. The court experience thereby becomes for Susanna "secondary victimization and re-traumatization."[27] It is only when they are separated that their power dissolves in the light of truth.

There is a painful element even within wise Daniel's questioning. As rabbi and scholar Dalia Marx points out, Daniel's statement to the elder that "beauty has seduced you, and lust has corrupted your heart" could be seen as tantamount to accusing her of being responsible for corrupting the elders.[28] What also struck me was the claim by Daniel that the elders had previously successfully used fear to do exactly the same to other women: "This is how you both have been dealing with the daughters of Israel, and they were intimate with you through fear; but a daughter of Judah would

---

26. Exum, "Fragmented Women," 197.
27. Smart, *Feminism and the Power of Law*, 26.
28. Marx, "Prayer of Susanna," 226.

not endure your wickedness." Such facts may have been unknown to this gathered community but now divinely revealed to Daniel. However, it is also well documented how many abusers whose known deeds are covered over, are still able to climb their career ladders whilst their victims are left behind hidden by silence. Why were they not brought to account long ago? Why were they allowed to continue and how on earth had they gained such high positions? These are questions that continue to devastate us today as so many perpetrators of abuse have continued to be promoted to influential positions, leaving a trail of destruction behind them in this same way. These are what I alluded to in the midrash as the "shadows of the crowd," the shadow side of institutions protecting themselves, and the shadows in our society. Our shadows embedded in structural injustice have allowed such violence to go unchecked for so long. Susanna's story begs us to be involved in revolutionizing the structures in our society today.

This chapter addresses a form of silence which is forced upon a person or community, and when, in turn, silence on behalf of the survivor becomes a means of survival. Situations of violence and abuse often result in silencing—the threat of retaliation if the victim speaks out, the experience of shame and (misplaced) guilt by the sufferer who then is paralyzed and unable to tell the horrific story, or when society through disbelief and blame forces silence upon the survivor. Contexts of war also involve enforced silences, either due to persecution, oppression of a culture and language, or eventually silencing by death itself.

The Susanna story can be seen as a resistance text, and a text that can give succor to others similarly afflicted. The book of Susanna along with the artwork available can be used as heuristic resources giving salutary lessons that Susanna would want all of us to hear. And it will be in the deep listening to Susanna that we will discover blessings, challenges, and gifts.

DANIEL 13:1–64[29]

Susanna's Beauty Attracts Two Elders

There was a man living in Babylon whose name was Joakim. [2] He married the daughter of Hilkiah, named Susanna, a very beautiful woman and one who feared the Lord. [3] Her parents were righteous, and had trained their daughter according to the law of Moses. [4] Joakim was very rich, and had a fine garden adjoining his house; the Jews used to come to him because he was the most honored of them all.

29. *New Revised Standard Version*, Catholic edition.

⁵ That year two elders from the people were appointed as judges. Concerning them the Lord had said: "Wickedness came forth from Babylon, from elders who were judges, who were supposed to govern the people." ⁶ These men were frequently at Joakim's house, and all who had a case to be tried came to them there.

⁷ When the people left at noon, Susanna would go into her husband's garden to walk. ⁸ Every day the two elders used to see her, going in and walking about, and they began to lust for her. ⁹ They suppressed their consciences and turned away their eyes from looking to Heaven or remembering their duty to administer justice. ¹⁰ Both were overwhelmed with passion for her, but they did not tell each other of their distress, ¹¹ for they were ashamed to disclose their lustful desire to seduce her. ¹² Day after day they watched eagerly to see her.

¹³ One day they said to each other, "Let us go home, for it is time for lunch." So they both left and parted from each other. ¹⁴ But turning back, they met again; and when each pressed the other for the reason, they confessed their lust. Then together they arranged for a time when they could find her alone.

The Elders Attempt to Seduce Susanna

¹⁵ Once, while they were watching for an opportune day, she went in as before with only two maids, and wished to bathe in the garden, for it was a hot day. ¹⁶ No one was there except the two elders, who had hidden themselves and were watching her. ¹⁷ She said to her maids, "Bring me olive oil and ointments, and shut the garden doors so that I can bathe." ¹⁸ They did as she told them: they shut the doors of the garden and went out by the side doors to bring what they had been commanded; they did not see the elders, because they were hiding.

¹⁹ When the maids had gone out, the two elders got up and ran to her. ²⁰ They said, "Look, the garden doors are shut, and no one can see us. We are burning with desire for you; so give your consent, and lie with us. ²¹ If you refuse, we will testify against you that a young man was with you, and this was why you sent your maids away."

²² Susanna groaned and said, "I am completely trapped. For if I do this, it will mean death for me; if I do not, I cannot escape your hands. ²³ I choose not to do it; I will fall into your hands, rather than sin in the sight of the Lord."

²⁴ Then Susanna cried out with a loud voice, and the two elders shouted against her. ²⁵ And one of them ran and opened the garden doors. ²⁶ When the people in the house heard the shouting in the garden, they rushed in at

the side door to see what had happened to her. [27] And when the elders told their story, the servants felt very much ashamed, for nothing like this had ever been said about Susanna.

The Elders Testify against Susanna

[28] The next day, when the people gathered at the house of her husband Joakim, the two elders came, full of their wicked plot to have Susanna put to death. In the presence of the people they said, [29] "Send for Susanna daughter of Hilkiah, the wife of Joakim." [30] So they sent for her. And she came with her parents, her children, and all her relatives.

[31] Now Susanna was a woman of great refinement and beautiful in appearance. [32] As she was veiled, the scoundrels ordered her to be unveiled, so that they might feast their eyes on her beauty. [33] Those who were with her and all who saw her were weeping.

[34] Then the two elders stood up before the people and laid their hands on her head. [35] Through her tears she looked up toward Heaven, for her heart trusted in the Lord. [36] The elders said, "While we were walking in the garden alone, this woman came in with two maids, shut the garden doors, and dismissed the maids. [37] Then a young man, who was hiding there, came to her and lay with her. [38] We were in a corner of the garden, and when we saw this wickedness, we ran to them. [39] Although we saw them embracing, we could not hold the man, because he was stronger than we are, and he opened the doors and got away. [40] We did, however, seize this woman and asked who the young man was, [41] but she would not tell us. These things we testify."

Because they were elders of the people and judges, the assembly believed them and condemned her to death.

[42] Then Susanna cried out with a loud voice, and said, "O eternal God, you know what is secret and are aware of all things before they come to be; [43] you know that these men have given false evidence against me. And now I am to die, though I have done none of the wicked things that they have charged against me!"

[44] The Lord heard her cry. [45] Just as she was being led off to execution, God stirred up the holy spirit of a young lad named Daniel, [46] and he shouted with a loud voice, "I want no part in shedding this woman's blood!"

Daniel Rescues Susanna

[47] All the people turned to him and asked, "What is this you are saying?" [48] Taking his stand among them he said, "Are you such fools, O Israelites, as to condemn a daughter of Israel without examination and without learning the facts? [49] Return to court, for these men have given false evidence against her."

[50] So all the people hurried back. And the rest of the[a] elders said to him, "Come, sit among us and inform us, for God has given you the standing of an elder." [51] Daniel said to them, "Separate them far from each other, and I will examine them."

[52] When they were separated from each other, he summoned one of them and said to him, "You old relic of wicked days, your sins have now come home, which you have committed in the past, [53] pronouncing unjust judgments, condemning the innocent and acquitting the guilty, though the Lord said, 'You shall not put an innocent and righteous person to death.' [54] Now then, if you really saw this woman, tell me this: Under what tree did you see them being intimate with each other?" He answered, "Under a mastic tree."[b] [55] And Daniel said, "Very well! This lie has cost you your head, for the angel of God has received the sentence from God and will immediately cut[b] you in two."

[56] Then, putting him to one side, he ordered them to bring the other. And he said to him, "You offspring of Canaan and not of Judah, beauty has beguiled you and lust has perverted your heart. [57] This is how you have been treating the daughters of Israel, and they were intimate with you through fear; but a daughter of Judah would not tolerate your wickedness. [58] Now then, tell me: Under what tree did you catch them being intimate with each other?" He answered, "Under an evergreen oak."[c] [59] Daniel said to him, "Very well! This lie has cost you also your head, for the angel of God is waiting with his sword to split[c] you in two, so as to destroy you both."

[60] Then the whole assembly raised a great shout and blessed God, who saves those who hope in him. [61] And they took action against the two elders, because out of their own mouths Daniel had convicted them of bearing false witness; they did to them as they had wickedly planned to do to their neighbor. [62] Acting in accordance with the law of Moses, they put them to death. Thus innocent blood was spared that day.

[63] Hilkiah and his wife praised God for their daughter Susanna, and so did her husband Joakim and all her relatives, because she was found innocent of a shameful deed. [64] And from that day onward Daniel had a great reputation among the people.

Footnotes

    a. Gk lacks *rest of the*

    b. The Greek words for *mastic tree* and *cut* are similar, thus forming an ironic wordplay

    c. The Greek words for *evergreen oak* and *split* are similar, thus forming an ironic wordplay

5

Selah: Slivers of Silence

BREATH

Are you looking for me? I am in the next seat.
My shoulder is against yours.
You will not find me in stupas, not in Indian shrine rooms,
nor in synagogues, nor in cathedrals:
not in masses, nor in kirtans, not in legs winding around your
own neck, nor in eating nothing but vegetables.
When you really look for me, you will see me instantly—
you will find me in the tiniest house of time.
Kabir says: Student, tell me what is God?
He is the breath inside the breath.[1]

*S*elah as found in the Psalms and Habakkuk. It is not easily translatable, but there is general agreement among Hebrew scholars that it may mean pause, wait, notice, or lift up. Its origins are uncertain, but it is also similar to an Arabic word meaning "connection." This chapter's focus is on the small

1. Bly, *Kabir: Ecstatic Poems*, 53.

pauses, *selah*s or, as Kabir puts it in the poem above, in the tiniest houses of time that we encounter in day-to-day life, which offer us a multitude of moments in which we may encounter God.

Every day of our life is sprinkled with these slivers of silence. Some of us live with more silence than others. Those who live on their own or in remote locations can feel they have too much silence. And yet under these circumstances, it can be easy to become deaf to the invitations of God. As we enter these moments in increasing frequency and with increasing depth, our lives may take on a greater contemplative way of being, opening a pathway to descend from our noisy heads into our hearts to pray without ceasing.

Beginning with Psalm 32, where I first took notice of this little word, this chapter also explores tiny *selah*s I encountered in a bookshop and at a concert. These slivers can become tiny houses of time that open their doors to us offering hospitality from the Divine who beckons us to come in, to taste, to see, to be in the company of God, who is host of the universe. As we enter these, we find just how expansive and spacious on the inside these tiny spaces can be.

TINIEST HOUSES OF TIME

The First Selah, Psalm 32:1–4[2]

Blessed is the one
    whose transgression is forgiven,
    whose sins are covered.
Blessed is the one
    whose sin the LORD does not count against them
    and in whose spirit there is no deceit.

When I kept silent,
    my bones wasted away
    through my groaning all day long.
For day and night
    your hand was heavy on me;
my strength was sapped
    as in the heat of summer.

Selah

---

2. Gateway Bible, *New International Version*, for quotations from Psalm 32 throughout this chapter.

It was a cold grey morning, the sun rising bleakly with little warmth through patchy cloud. I lit a candle, turned to the reading set for the day, Psalm 32, and began to read. "Blessed is the one whose transgression is forgiven": I could feel this touching on something I had been carrying, that sick feeling in the pit of my stomach that tells me not all is right. What was this about? My body alerted me first, before my self-justifying mind would let me see it: those comments that were hurtful that I spoke out so quickly before thinking about the pain these words inflicted. My wise body that does not lie revealed to me what I didn't want to know. But here it was, unaddressed and welling up within me. And then more—from years back where I hurt loved ones with some specific actions when I was a teenager. Things buried for so very long now all rose to the surface. "When I kept silent, my bones withered away," verse 3 said. But determined and resistant, I ploughed on.

After verse 4, I noticed and then passed over the strange word, *selah*. I hadn't taken too much notice of this tiny word before and so this time I just kept reading. But my eyes continued returning to this mysterious little word. Could it be my eyes telling me I had missed something—something vital? What could this one word have to offer? I looked it up in the concordance, which told me it was given as a directive to the musician, origin unclear, and probable meaning is "to pause or wait." So, I waited with this little slip of a word and, listening to its sound rolling around in my mind, it sounded a bit like a sigh.

After a short while, it was as if *selah* was lowering me down into my own center. It reminded me of the few times when I went caving and abseiled with the safety of rope down into a pothole. Landing at the bottom of the cavity, I continued through what cavers refer to as a squeeze: a very narrow tight space that I had to crawl through on my stomach, pushing my helmet in front of me. It was as if I was being threaded through my own eye of a needle. And *selah* now was my rope of safety as I slowly moved through this tunnel of time and space, from my head into my heart's center, deeper and deeper. I recalled the words of the psalm I had just read, "Blessed is the one . . . Blessed is the one . . . ," a gentle rhythmic repetition with my heartbeat. This I wanted, to feel and know blessedness deep in the marrow of my bones and in the core of my stomach; to be freed from the heaviness and churning of my unfaced wrong.

Selah: listen, wait in the silence.

Surrounded by pressing darkness, it was the double beatitude, the twice repeated "blessed is," that encouraged me not to flee and take the easy way out. I inched my way deeper in, breathing in *selah*, and breathing out *selah*; breathing in the Spirit, and breathing out my fear.

As I descended, the atmosphere became cooler, denser. My stomach continued its roiling and swirling, taking me close to feeling nauseous. I wasn't ready for this. How contrite do I need to be before it is considered a confession—a pure and contrite heart you will not turn away (Ps 51:17). The veins in my body pumped with turbulence, confusion; . . . should I wait until I am sorrier, more contrite, sad, regretful? Anyway, could I ever be sorry enough? And is confession an admission, like the admission at the entry to Australia's Jenolan Caves? Admission opens the way to go in, to push against the turnstile and move in to see what is there in the darkness. A bit like going down into Churchill's bunker, I felt the shadows of war and strategy, defence and resistance, attacking and feinting. My soul was like a withered snakeskin, empty, fragile, dry, and thin. My legs trembled as I felt my way forward through this gritty darkness.

Oh, I had been living well enough in the thin light of previous confessions and forgivenesses, pretending all was fine. But deep inside this caverned heart was a groaning, heavy sadness. I had begun to wither away in my hidden folds of quilted guilt, soft and wrapped in a counterfeit comfort hiding from myself. Self-deception: how pervasive this is; it is in the air I breathe, the things I think, the way I speak, cheating me of the deeper comfort of truth, and the rich light of confessed wrong.

I reached the end of the long squeeze, and felt the airiness of a huge underground cavern that was opening out before me. Descending through the tiniest house of time I began to look around this underground chamber. I could smell the dankness, the cloying darkness, the bat droppings, and I was blinded by the darkness. This was part of me, of my own heart. Silence: a dreadful thick silence and darkness. I could see my own breath as I breathed out *selah* into the cold air. I knelt down, knowing this was where I needed to be, and with a deep desire growing now to let go of all my stumbling wrongdoing. I waited. And waited. A warm draft, almost imperceptible, much like the sweet-smelling breezes that whisper, "Spring is coming," fingered its way through my hair like a parent's reassuring caress. I breathed in this warmth, and remembered Kabir's promise that Presence is the "breath inside the breath"! In the midst of my apprehension the Spirit was apprehending me! God was here in this tiny dark house encouraging and guiding with a hospitality ready to receive my confessions. I drew courage.

I looked down and saw I was holding large lumps of conglomerate rock in this underground cavity of my heart: Bits of hard quartz-like resentment stuck unspoken to a lump of crumbly envy; a black basalt clast holding a dark awareness of a recent conversation, where my ego triumphed with a shard-like comment over my true self. Geological detritus held together by the crudely stratified layers of my tendency to depend on myself rather than on God. Heavy, wearying, and very uncomfortable. As I acknowledged it all, named it and owned it, I had imagined I would have to dig it out of my heart as a miner would hack away at the rockface. But as I spoke it out, it seemed to tumble so easily out of me and land on the rubble floor. It was no longer part of me—I was light, with a wondrous interior spaciousness. Only God can dissipate the darkness. So quickly did I feel the forgiveness and lightness from God that I could hardly remember the heaviness. It seemed to take me so very long to get to this point, and yet it was so quick to suddenly receive this lightness of being.

The Second Selah, Psalm 32:5–7a

Then I acknowledged my sin to you
    and did not cover up my iniquity.
I said, "I will confess
    my transgressions to the LORD."
And you forgave
    the guilt of my sin.

                                                Selah

Therefore let all the faithful pray to you
    while you may be found;
surely the rising of the mighty waters
    will not reach them.
You are my hiding place;
    you will protect me from trouble

And so, with great relief and release, I continued to read the psalm slowly. Coming to this second *selah*, I paused, read on, and then returned and breathed again, in and out, *selah*. *Selah*: my agent of transport back into my heart where God resides, and this time I felt the flight of joy within my bones. A kind of childlike levity seemed to lift me up and propel me down the slippery-slide of my childhood memory in the local park. It was a huge slippery-slide, shiny and metal and warmed by the sun, and at the bottom a sandpit caught me as I landed helter-skelter in laughter. This time, the tiny house of time took me to a childhood tree house in a secret wild garden. A playful place free from trouble, where I am guileless again for a moment; forgiven, and filled with wonder and trust. I could see the Spirit leaning against the trunk of the huge tree with the rickety little tree house perched high in its branches. As I settled into the grooves of the tree roots, I could feel the shoulder of God next to mine and a deep contentedness enfolded me. And gratitude too, for such love that forgives and releases, unbinds and drops off the boulders I needlessly lug from one day into the next. I recalled a recent walk through the forest near where I was living, where I had stopped at the foot of a huge oak tree. Someone had placed a tiny door about eight inches high between two large roots, which opened into the trunk of the tree. How could I not smile in wonder and daydream into the magic and mystery of a child's imagination? Such awe and curiosity that as an adult I can lose so quickly.

I dug my fingers into the earth—rich humus, whose smell speaks of life-in-the-making. The ethnobiologist Dr. Robin Wall Kimmerer talks about the Potawatomi word that describes the life force that pushes a mushroom up from darkness into the light: *puhpowee*. She remarks that science has no word for this mystery; science has names for what is known, but not for the enigmas, riddles, and secrets such as this sudden bursting forth overnight of new life.[3] I thought then that perhaps this mystery I had experienced, the sudden bursting forth out of the dark cold cave of unconfessed heaviness into this life-light of forgiveness, was indeed an experience of *puhpowee*.

The Third Selah, Psalm 32:7b–11

As if my ears had become unblocked, I became aware for the first time of the birds chattering at the window feeder. *I* was becoming unblocked. I turned again to the psalm.

> You shall surround me with songs of deliverance
>
> *Selah*
>
> I will instruct you and teach you in the way you should go;
>   I will counsel you with my loving eye on you.
> Do not be like the horse or the mule,
>   which have no understanding,
> but must be controlled by bit and bridle
>   or they will not come to you.
> Many are the woes of the wicked,
>   But the LORD's unfailing love
>   surrounds the one who trusts in him.
> Rejoice in the LORD and be glad, you righteous;
>   sing, all you who are upright in heart!

3. Kimmerer, *Braiding Sweet Grass*.

"You shall surround me with songs of deliverance." Perhaps the bird-song was the heralding of deliverance for me, and not only me but also for the whole world. After the *selah*, the voice of the psalmist addressing God changes to God speaking to me, the reader. It was as if I wouldn't have been ready to hear God until the ringing in my own ears of sin reverberating like an echo chamber of my own ego's striving had been dealt with. And I needed to find that moment of sitting in the presence of God, transported by *selah* into wonder and trust, receptivity and alertness.

It happened with such ease this time. I slid seamlessly through *selah* into the tiny slice of time's silence, and found myself swimming in soft light. *I will guide you with my eye* were the words that resonated for me, becoming my focus and paving the way of descent into my heart. I rested in that soft light. I began to gaze into the eyes of God. And God was gazing into mine. How could this be, this mortal me gazing into the eyes of Infinity; my faltering, fleeting love encountering Perfect Love; my small moment in time interlocking with the One who is Eternal and outside time; my cloudy vision being met by the All-seeing One who promises to guide me with this eye of Love? And was that my reflection I was seeing in the eye of God?

I sensed a merging, that feeling of I-am-in-God-and-God-is-in-me, looking into God and God looking into me, as if I was being taken up into the very eye of God—a deep sea of emeralds and blues, of infinite depth and color. I was being swept into the vast ocean of God's eye, into the rounded-ness of a cradling watery hemisphere that seemed to sparkle and twinkle, incandescent with joy and laughter. Deep calling to deep. Immersed and wet all over, I could breathe under water. I played and plunged down into this ocean, floating, swirling, submerged and free. The water was cool, crystal clear, and the light danced in blue-green luminescent patterns like minia-ture starbursts. At that moment I was filled with a dancing light. This invita-tion had come from God, and this tiniest house of time had transported me into the home of God's eye. A place where I could look with God's own vision and be shown what my eyes alone could not and cannot see: beyond my eye's ability to articulate, and my mind's ability to grasp. Something of the beauty and beyond-ness of God flooded my whole being. This was like tumbling and swimming in a swirling world of liquid light and love: the world of God who is the Source of all light and love; the Living Water, the One in whom all things hold together. The emerald-blue currents lifted and carried me, until I was swept into another current and cradled in the arms of Mother God as she swayed her fluid way through time and space, her tender eyes wandering the earth and cherishing all she beheld. I was being held, cherished, within her eye, within her loving beholding gaze guiding me deeper into Love.

Selah in an Antiquarian Bookshop

"Pockets of God" are everywhere! In "guttery gaps," in a "cut-away bog" and mystery touches through "a crumb of bread."[4] I was sitting on the floor, curled up against the base of a floor-to-ceiling wooden bookcase somewhere in the huge rabbit-warren bookshop that specialised in rare, antique, and secondhand books. The comparatively recent book, *Collected Poems* by Patrick Kavanagh, was open on my lap, and these were his words tumbling from the pages, speaking to me about the tiny pockets and tiny houses in which we can encounter the Divine. There were some faint pencil marks underlining words and scribbled down the margins from a previous owner of the book, mostly too faint to read, but wonderful to know I had company sitting between these pages, whispering their comments in the silences between the lines.

This open book sat like cupped hands before me, like a crucible holding golden words that twinkled and shone, alive on the page. As I read, I felt the gold was spreading into the air like children's sparkle dust. This was just one book I was sitting with, among all the thousands of precious vertical gold ingots of books, slotted in side by side, row after row, shelf after shelf, each holding words and worlds of storied moments. The gold dust of God is in all things, and then also in all non-things, in the spaces and silences between all things, between all books, in cupped hands and between pages, between the lines, and between each sentence when one ends and before the next begins.

Patrick Kavanagh, the wonderful Irish mystic and poet, now deceased, was speaking across distant layers of times and landscapes. He could see so clearly how extravagantly God fills every nook and cranny of time and space with invitations of hospitality. God was walking among the books and people here too. And each of Kavanagh's words was chosen with such care. I began to reflect: How often do I speak without care, either for the specific words, or sometimes carelessly without regard for someone I love? At times I have found myself using words and filling spaces without aim or purpose; perhaps to disguise the fact that I don't know what I think or when I know nothing about a topic.

I became aware of the silences around me—more than just a single silence. There seemed to be shades of silences, and it was as if the Word of all words was lingering on the inside of these tiny houses of silence and catching my attention, enticing me to make the effort and knock on the door of

---

4. A selection of phrases from Kavanagh, *Collected Poems*; "pockets of God" from the poem, "The Long Garden"; "guttery gaps" and " a crumb of bread" from the poem, "The Great Hunger"; and "cut-away bog" from the poem, "The One."

a little house. I was tired, and I knew we did not have much time left in this store. I could so easily ignore this gentle nudge and keep reading. It took a few moments of back-and-forth debate with myself to decide to surrender to this gentle invitation. I looked at my watch (I couldn't help myself) and then took a few deep breaths. I thought I would try, almost half-heartedly.

Slowly I became more conscious of the musty inky smell around me of old paper, wood shelving, and leather-bound volumes. The soft crumble of well-used spines seemed to emit their own form of silence. The yellowed typeset pages where many readers had left traces of their emotions and thoughts trailing between the lines or scribbled in the margins all lay now in silence. These book aromas enveloped me, inviting me also into their antique-filled spaces. And here, on the floor and between bookcases, I was being beckoned, by this "beautiful, beautiful, beautiful God"[5] of Patrick's who was breathing through the shelves and spaces.

What treasures must lie within all these books, I wondered, and what stories did they hold, not only of their own, but compounded with those of their owners and readers over time? I looked down, noticing the shine from the polished floorboards. They also had their cracks and joins and, as I peered down from this third level, the light from level two below shone through one of the cracks. I could hear the slow creaking of careful footsteps as people reverently crept their way between the corridors and multilayered levels of books and time. Next to me, piled high on the floor, were my gatherings from the past hours of wandering in this hall of authors, a possible selection of the cheaper and not-very-old secondhand books that I could afford. On my way I had stopped before an untouchable deep olive, leather-bound, gold-gilded 1806 set of Shakespeare's plays in a glass case. I had breathed in the fragile texture of a rusty-red frayed fabric-bound first edition of *Alice's Adventures in Wonderland*, with its swirled endpapers and feathered pages. But I needed to turn my attention back again to God in the silences. I retuned my ears to listen to the sounds of silent cherished volumes in greens, reds, and golds; the slow ponderous movements of customers; the gravitas of carefully catalogued treasures; the rich powdery dust hanging in the stillness of the air.

I leaned my head against the bookcase and closed my eyes. Yes, the soft, downy Presence was here without doubt. "Come in! Come in!" God's voice was quiet, cajoling, almost jocular. The indulgent generosity of a gracious Father and Mother seemed to attract me. I was drawn in and embraced in this small moment: a paper-thin page of time. The feathery presence seemed to expand and fill the whole space in which I was sitting. Subtle, light, wispy

5. Kavanagh, *Collected Poems*; from the poem, "The One."

thin and yet strong like silk spun by a silkworm, wrapping me in its golden presence. I began to feel an indescribable gratitude to God for the generosity of such a moment; for the poet and lover of God that Patrick had been and the gifts of wisdom he had left us; and for all the richness of how the Word creates words. Sheer gossamer gift. And so I sat in that tiny house of time and silence. Cocooned. Captivated.

Attending a Concert with Selah

Selah had now become like a personal friend, a personification of these slivers of time that are everywhere in every context, like small silent chapels of time inserted into moments through the day; like a sacred architecture of time shaping spaces for entry into the holy of holies. Each one a door through which to encounter the Divine.

One evening we were at Angel Place Concert Hall in Sydney (a fitting name for such musical events!), where Richard Tognetti, an Australian violinist, composer, and conductor, was to be playing on a violin claimed to have been owned originally by Paganini himself. What could be more exquisite? I had always enjoyed Richard's playing, and this night we were only a few rows from the stage.

The concert was about to begin. We had applauded the orchestra onto the stage and instruments were tuned, followed by Richard striding in gracefully on the exuberantly warm greetings of the audience. Here he was as always—director, arranger and daring de-ranger, conductor and idiosyncratic soloist all in one. The lights dimmed, the shuffling ceased, and the last cough was muffled. Richard lifted his violin to his chin, and held his bow, poised.

Silence. Such a full silence, soft and thick—*selah* was here indeed. Not a muscle moved. The stillness was palpable, quelling; every fibre of being in the hall was focused, and expectation hung spread-eagled in the air. What sound was this—the sound our silence together was making as an audience this night?

Then Richard drew in a deep breath, and the first notes were sent sparking into the air. The fabric of the silence seemed to be set aflame leaving a shimmer of color and texture as if it had its own goose bumps. And there I felt and heard a sister to *selah*: the fermata, 𝄐 that musical "grand pause" or "hold" peering like an eagle's eye over the silences depicted on the score as if it had a bird's-eye view of moments suspended, miniature gestations, inviting us to be present at the births of living silences.

Claude Debussy apparently said that the music is not in the notes, but in the silences between. I wondered about all the little "silences between" that must lie quietly, waiting in the wings for their turn to be heard. These slivers of silence that glint like clear glass could take up the story of the notes on either side of them and offer up small windows through which to see a greater story, the bigger picture, the significance of perspective.

That night, Paganini's vibrant and ebullient music opened out for me silences within his music that carried some of that vividness and energy, and danced me into spacious silences with the Spirit.

The concert ran on, like a musical maypole of lightness and sheer fun, until finally only the last piece of the night was to be played: Vivaldi's "Spring." Richard's violin—a 1743 *Carrodus* referred to as a *del Gesu* made only twenty years after Vivaldi composed the *Four Seasons*—seemed to make all the walls of the hall resonate and ring. Vivaldi's "Spring" was coming to the end. The final bar.

And then silence. A silence that became a great silence, making its regal entrance, holding airborne the last chords like a royal train. Richard's bow remained aloft, hovering and still holding this last silent note: beautiful, weighty, mysterious, momentous . . . then moving into an enraptured awe of silence. Richard's arm slowly came down, and the thunder began: at first a slow rumbling of clapping and calls for more, followed by feet pounding on the floor until all the audience was standing, acclaiming the wonder of majestic music and silences played magnificently. This last silence, this *selah*, was full of the wondrous presence of the God of all creativity, and my face was wet with tears.

REFLECTION

Psalmic Pauses

I have read the Psalms for years, but had ever taken any notice of this quaint little word—*selah*—sitting quietly, intermittently among the stanzas. Three times Psalm 32 invites us to stop, and weigh up what we have heard. To sit in the silence while the hook on the end of the line drops deeper and deeper into our souls, to catch what is there, and offer it up for attention. When I later researched music recordings of this psalm, I did not find one rendition that expressed these three *selah*s in any apparent way. It seems I wasn't the only one ignoring this enigmatic invitation to silence.

The psalm begins by pointing to the blessedness of a state of being where we are free from carrying the bundle of our hurts, wrongs, resentments, and our ego's demands. This is a possibility for all of us that glows with attractiveness. It is a summons toward wholeness. Then the brutal honesty of the psalmist's own experience of the slow death-like destruction of unconfessed wrong is expressed, which may be a part of the psalm that we want to steer clear of. But the *selah* encourages us to stop, take stock, and listen to our souls. Many of us wrestle with the concept of sin. It is an unfashionable concept many don't like mentioning.

We can be so subtly invaded by an unhealthy understanding of sin and service, which means we don't consider our own needs but feel we need to serve others at all times, often to the detriment of our own health; and if we have a desire not to do so this can be experienced as the sin of selfishness. This misconception still has its echoes particularly among women who struggle to take time out for themselves, for their health, or even for prayer and retreats, considering that to do so is to be self-centered. It is an essential and liberating exercise that many have taken up, to voice dissidence, explore new ways of seeing God, freedom, holiness, and sin. This exploration means in particular re-examining concepts of sin for women.

It is also vital that we become aware of ways in which we have been sinned against, or made to be scapegoats. For some, such an awareness encourages healthy shifts in theologies and churches, moving to where structural and institutional evil is acknowledged, and sin recognized as both individual and corporate, including structural oppression. The feminist views of sin can offer a deeply empowering movement of a community of people whose desire is mutuality-in-relationships. It is liberating to recognize that sin is not about being driven into guilt and the downward spiral of self-abnegation. Rather, it is working with one's sin to identify those things holding us back from becoming our best selves, from becoming fully alive and being able to receive the generosity of God's love. This includes noticing those things that stifle a deeper relationship with the Divine, with others, with our own selves, and with creation. Salvation then becomes allowing the false self to fall away and entering into one's true self as created in the image of the Divine.

We have much to learn from Julian of Norwich (1342–1416), author, mystic, and wise spiritual counsellor, who offered a theology regarding sin and the mothering of God that was radically different from that of most of her contemporaries, and continues to help us today to shift our assumptions and perspectives when life is extremely challenging. Julian was alive during a time of great poverty and famine, when waves of the plague swept Europe. As an anchoress, she was confined to her small cell attached to the Church of St. Julian, and thus experienced her own voluntary self-isolation. This enabled her to spend her time in prayer, offering spiritual guidance, and writing what she received from God. It is estimated that around one third of the population died due to the plague just in Julian's own region, and it is highly probable that from her cell she—along with most of the townsfolk—would have been able to smell the burning of the bodies of those who had succumbed to the plague. In the midst of this pandemic, she offered a profoundly hope-filled theology, and challenged the prevailing assumption that God was wrathful, punishing everyone for their sin. Instead, she proclaimed that God was not angry, but rather understood the frailty of humanity and their capacity to sin. And although God had every right to be angry, according to Julian, God was instead full of great love and tender compassion, and it is this love that so captivates us that we are drawn to be reconciled again and again with Jesus. "In falling and in rising we are ever preciously kept in one Love,"[6] she says. This loving God, according to Julian, is both mother and father, and she points out the mothering acts that Jesus performs in his care of us.[7] Sheila Upjohn, one of the most prolific writers and speakers on Julian, reflects on the continued relevance of Julian's teaching, and writes, "It is a spurious humility that makes our own hatred of ourselves more important than Christ's love for us."[8]

The second *selah* enabled me to notice the bodily impact of having received forgiveness and release. Sometimes we can know theoretically that we are forgiven, but struggle to feel that in our gut. I have found, in my work as a spiritual director guiding those following the Ignatian Exercises, that it is very helpful for retreatants to be able to be attentive to both head knowledge (*saber*, in Spanish), as well as a bodily or "felt sense" knowledge, for which Ignatius uses the Spanish word *sentir*. *Sentir* is the wisdom of the body, that source of knowledge that has its own language of communication, telling us what words cannot express, and often communicating to us an under-story that we could so easily miss. Ignatius continually points out that *sentir* is an important source of wisdom for discernment, as we seek to pay attention to the movements of the Spirit within us. Just as we can know—*saber*—that we are unconditionally loved by God, we can also know—*sentir*—that we have doubts that this is really true. There may be circumstances or triggers where we find ourselves feeling bereft of the love of God, yet knowing rationally that nothing can separate us from the love of God (Rom 8:39). Once we acknowledge what our bodies are telling us, we can partner with the Spirit to move toward transformation, renewal, and being able to engage in life anew from the inside out.

6. Julian of Norwich, *Revelations of Divine Love*, 197.
7. Obbard, *Through Julian's Window*.
8. Upjohn, *Why Julian Now?* 69.

The Syriac New Testament expresses the embodiment of this aliveness in a fresh way. According to Elizabeth Rees,[9] instead of the phrases "to deliver," "to redeem," and "to save," indicating the need to be *taken from* something, the Syriac verbs of "to give life," "to make alive," and "to cause to live" suggest we are *gifted into* something. This gifting into life is—to use the Potawatomi word—the *puhpowee* I experienced, the new life that sprang up like a mushroom so surprisingly and wondrously. As the psalmist knew so well, new life is indeed "blessed."

The third *selah* takes us into the deep ocean of God's beholding of us in unconditional love. When Jesus said to the disciples to "put out into the deep water" (Luke 5:4), it is this deep water of God's presence that we can be plunged into. It was Meister Eckhart who said, "The eye with which we see God is the same with which God sees me. My eye and God's eye is one eye, and one sight, and one knowledge, and one love."[10] This is the eye of Love, the watchful caring of Creator God who birthed the earth and all that is in it. We can fear being seen—fully seen as we are—by others and also by God. We can tolerate the long loving look of someone we love and with whom we have deep trust, yet even with them, we often find there comes a point at which we begin to feel uncomfortable. The intimacy of such long-held regarding of us can feel too intimate, too vulnerable, too revealing. Yet this unconditional, intimate love of God is one of the things we most yearn for, while at the same time we fear it. At this point it is helpful to turn again to the ethnobiologist Kimmerer, who brings a very grounded and helpful perspective to being closely gazed upon by Mother God. In her book, *Braiding Sweetgrass*, she refers to research that suggests the scent of humus releases oxytocin, which is the same hormone emitted when a mother and child gaze into each other's eyes, facilitating the bonding between mother and child. Secreted by the hypothalamus, oxytocin is often referred to as the "love hormone" or the "bonding hormone." And there are current medical studies examining the role of oxytocin administered to reduce the effects of post-traumatic stress.[11] Here is gentle encouragement for us. As we make our way prayerfully through the stanzas of the psalms, like fingering the beads in a rosary separated by threads of *selah*-spaces, can we allow this oxytocin be released and felt in our bodies? Can we be vulnerable enough to receive the Mothering God watching over us—as we swim in the oceans, cradled in the eye of Love; as we dig deep into the earthy humus that gives life to trees and to the mushrooms, now bestowing on us the *puhpowee* life-giving

9. Rees, *Early Christianity*, 46.

10. Eckhart, *Seven Sermons*, 24.

11. Van Zuiden et al., "Intranasal Oxytocin."

lift; as we notice our own breath that breathes deeply the loamy smell that releases a hormone that bonds mother and child? And we can experience this infilling of love again and again, like circling the beads in a rosary. This circling moves outwards, as we carry into the world the capacity to receive love, which transforms our postures from one who is fearful to one who is beloved. We then carry this stance into our communities as we take the holy journey of learning more and more authentically how to love others unconditionally.

To be seen deeply by God, to be beheld by this Mothering Spirit, is to be transformed and even transfigured. Only God can affect such deep shifts, and it may all happen within such a sliver of time: in the twinkling of an eye. And yet it doesn't end there. We are always transformed not only for ourselves, but for how we are in the world, who we are with others, and what we are partnering in with God.

Gold in the Silences between Pages

My husband and I love finding small inexpensive antique books whenever we can. One day we had driven some way to a bookstore specializing in antique, rare, and secondhand books. Always on the lookout for a bargain, we had decided to spend a few hours wandering the rows and floors of bookcases. Our habit was to split up, and we each would browse the treasures and, towards the end of our time, come together again and share what we had found; perhaps buying one small thing, or perhaps not. Towards the end of the time we had allotted this particular day, I had settled onto the floor with some of my gleanings and I was particularly thrilled to have found one of Patrick Kavanagh's collections—a poet to whom a dear Irish friend had introduced me some years ago.

Kavanagh (1904–67) was born in rural County Monaghan, part of the border region in Ireland. Leaving school at the age of twelve, and working for his shoemaker and farmer father, he began writing poetry and discovering his own way into writing literature. He was a complex character and, despite moving to Dublin later to further his writing career, there seems a sense in which he remained a border-dweller most of his life. Written from the edges of society, his God was not found in the mortar of cathedrals, but instead had an organic presence, being found in the mud and grasses, hills and ploughed fields. And Kavanagh's place to pray was not within four walls of a church building, but rather in the world of landscape and skies. Without the training in literature that can stipulate conventions and become confining, he developed his own, as if he were tutored by nature and the very culture in which he was embedded.

Assuming I would simply spend the time flipping through the book and devouring a poem here and a poem there, I had been taken by surprise by the sudden awareness of how Kavanagh's words were beguiling, luring me into the silences around me. Kavanagh's poetry reinforces the capacity to encounter the Presence of the Infinite One through a tiny finite object or moment. This enabled him to see the "beautiful, beautiful, beautiful God" that breathes in and through all places. The commas between these three words enable us to receive each "beautiful"—not simply as empty repetition, but as spacious layering of beauty. Commas, spaces, and pauses in writing have their own narratives we can listen to.

Silence is a literary device and we see silences portrayed spatially in the way lines in a poem or a speech are written, affecting the way we read, giving moments of pause as we move from one line mid-sentence to another. These *selah*s can be found in so many places, each proffering a tiny pocket in which we may encounter the Divine, the God of Silences.

Silence: The Carrier of Divine Music

The concert experience made me want to explore the role of silences in music, these musical *selah*s, and how they might enable me to enter more deeply into intimacy and encounter with the Divine. I listen to quite a lot of music, but I had not paid much attention to the music's silences. Who specifically uses silence in their compositions, and to what effect?

My first stop was to knock on Arvo Pärt's door. A contemporary Estonian composer who has gained great popularity recently, Pärt speaks about how he "had to draw this music gently out of silence and emptiness."[12] His music changed radically after a period of eight years of almost complete silence due to a spiritual encounter. Shifting from atonal music, Pärt's music became influenced by the Orthodox Church as well as the importance of silence, and "bears the promise of simplicity, purity and silence," writes Bouteneff. "Such stillness is readily associated with a purgative if not a cathartic aspect of spirituality[,] . . . a cleansing of all the noise that surrounds us as well as our own inner noise."[13]

Knocking on other doors, I came across Arthur Schnabel, an Austrian composer (1882–1951), who made the fascinating comment that the notes he played were not so much the issue, but rather it was the pauses between

12. Bouteneff, *Arvo Pärt: Out of Silence*, 19.
13. Bouteneff, *Arvo Pärt: Out of Silence*, 28.

notes, where he remarked that this is where the art resides! This reminded me of one of my favorite books, *Piano Lessons*, by the Australian pianist Anna Goldsworthy. Mrs. Sivan was Anna's Russian-born piano teacher who, in her expressive Russian English, constantly urged Anna to take note of silences: "This is first arts of any music: learn to listen to silence, atmospheric silence. Only then can we understand future and perspective," she said. "We must hear the sound before [the note]."[14] And as Anna was guided to play into the depths of each note instead of just playing the surface of the keys, she describes being able to play a "joy into my sounds, which no longer crashed to the ground, self-defeated, but reached out into the audience in thanksgiving, saying things otherwise unavailable."[15]

I also approached one of my favorite composers, Patrick Hawes, a contemporary English creator of numinous and prayerful music. Emailing him, I asked what role silence played in his creative process of composing. His gracious response included the following:

> Silence is to a musician what a blank canvas is to an artist or a block of stone to a sculptor. It is the starting point, the very beginning of a new creation. Therefore, it is always present—like the stone that is to be carved or the canvas which bears the paint. In other words, silence is the foundation of a piece of music and must be treated with the utmost respect. . . . Silence is the carrier of music. It lovingly provides the yoke for music to travel to its listeners. It is omni-present yet only occasionally discerned. The more it is discerned, the more powerful its presence becomes to the point that it can speak more loudly than sound. . . . Above all else, a composer must ensure that silence lives.[16]

This silence-that-lives-in-the-*selah*s was within the music of Vivaldi that night at Angel Place. This too was a tiny house of God-filled joy bursting out through the tiny houses of silence in the music, and then culminating with the great silence at the end. This for me was an awe-filled, worshipful silence of the Composer of all heavenly music. It could simply have been an emotional moment, a good experience, a "moving performance." But with an intentional awareness, it moved the experience toward a recognition of a deeper Truth, and deeper Reality; to the Composer behind all composers. And wasn't Tognetti's violin called a *del Gesu*?

14. Goldsworthy, *Piano Lessons*, 174.
15. Goldsworthy, *Piano Lessons*, 174.
16. Hawes, personal communication, April 25, 2019.

PONDERING YOUR OWN EXPERIENCES

- "*Selah* had now become like a personal friend, a personification of these slivers of time that are everywhere in every context, like small silent chapels of time inserted into moments through the day." Is there a psalm in the Bible that has *selah* within it, that you would like to ponder, allowing the word to pave the way for you to descend with the psalmist's words from your mind to your heart?

- "This invitation had come from God, and this tiniest house of time had transported me into the home of God's eye." Have you noticed some of the tiniest houses of time within the midst of your very busy days? You may like to experiment with entering into these "pockets of God" and encountering the Spirit.

- "I leaned my head against the bookcase and closed my eyes. Yes, the soft, downy Presence was here without doubt. . . . I was drawn in and embraced in this small moment: a paper-thin page of time." A bookshop can be a place where we are not simply hurrying in to buy a book and leave as soon as possible but, like anywhere we go, we can enter into the unique *selah*-spaces found in that place. The grocery store can offer a similar experience, where we can stand among the fruits and vegetables and, in a moment of silent contemplation, breathe in their distinct flavors and histories, notice the vibrant and muted colors, textures, and shapes. As you pause in the midst of such a harvest, where might the portals be for you to sink into the presence of God?

- If you do any writing—creative or otherwise—what do you notice about spaces and silences in and through the page? What conversations might you want to have with these? What is the hospitality being offered you by God in and through them?

- "The lights dimmed, the shuffling ceased, and the last cough was muffled. Richard lifted his violin to his chin, and held his bow, poised. Silence . . . *Selah* was here indeed." Is there some music that you like to listen to, a play or a performance that you might attend, where you can notice the different qualities of silence, and enter these moments like portals into the Presence of God? If you play or write music yourself, what invitations do the *selah* moments offer you?

FOR FURTHER ENGAGEMENT

Selah and Behold: Portals of Silence

As already mentioned, there is little agreement and much discussion around the meaning of *selah*. It has a composite etymology, resulting in the same word rarely being found in another context. The suggestions for the interpretation of the word range from a time to shout out, and exalt; to lift up; a time to weigh or weigh up (as in weighing gold). What seems to have the most consensus is that it was a musical term with some kind of instruction to the musicians. There are suggestions that it is a liturgical note requiring worshipers to become silent and to reflect on the psalmist's words,[17] or an array of meanings including lifting up voices, lifting up eyes, or an interlude in which to recite a benediction.[18] For the purposes of this book, *selah* has been interpreted along the lines of the latter suggestions. Perhaps due to the ambiguity surrounding the term, most musicians seem have chosen to ignore its presence in the recordings made of Psalm 32 that are available. Curiosity calls us to ask: Why is the word there? What might its gift be to us?

The word "behold" is a word that also calls us to pause, stop, and take in what is there before us. It breaks into our lives and halts us. And like *selah*, this word has also been largely ignored over recent years. Dan Schrock, in a presentation at the Anabaptist Mennonite Biblical Seminary in 2018 that I attended, pointed out that this word appears more than thirteen hundred times in Scripture. Its frequency is found by tracing the Hebrew, *henneh* or *chazah* and Greek, *idou*. Yet most modern translations seem either to ignore the word completely and so leave it out, or to offer "suddenly," "look," or "see." To be prompted to "look" is very different from being invited to "behold." Maggie Ross, an Anglican solitary and theologian living in Oxford, opens up the biblical concept of "behold" as a vast portal into silence and encounter with God.[19]

"Behold" comes from two root words meaning "thoroughly" and "to hold." This evokes a stance whereby one holds thoroughly what one notices. It suggests to the reader that there is a need to cease reading for a moment, wait, and draw into oneself the truth of what is being communicated. I would suggest that the recent (mis)translations reflect our own context: the busyness and speed with which we live means the call to behold just doesn't seem to fit. It's an anachronism best left behind. Silence, stopping, and beholding are indeed foreign to a culture that reveres speed-reading

---

17. Richards, *Global Concise Bible Dictionary*, 495.

18. Gehman, *New Westminster Dictionary*, 845.

19. Ross, *Silence: A User's Guide.*

and fast living. There is no time, no value in beholding what can be glanced at, flicked through, filed, and forgotten. Or, we can choose to read slowly and, as we do so, we begin to see deeply with the eyes of our heart.

We can skim across the top of life and skid across the surface of the word of God, or we can be halted by two small yet momentous words. The Russian mystic, Theophany the Recluse (1815–94), said, "To pray is to descend with the mind into the heart, and there to stand before the face of the Lord, ever-present, all-seeing, within you."[20] Both *selah* and "behold" proffer portals through which we can come before the face of God, where we can plumb the depths of our relationship with God and with ourselves. They open safe and courageous rooms where we can immerse ourselves in the transforming and transfiguring presence of this God who is found in and through every sliver of silence in Scriptures, poetry, creation, and everyday things—even shops.

A Pause among Books and Words

Ignatian spirituality often refers to God as being found in everything, just as Kavanagh does in his poetry, claiming that "God is in the bits and pieces of Everyday."[21] This is not to say Kavanagh or Ignatius can be accused of pantheism. It is clear from their writings that God can be found in everything, but God is not everything. This is a profligate God who extravagantly pours Presence into everything and every space; every moment of time and every experience. The presence of the Spirit, of *Ruach*, is all around us and within us, there for us to discover if we have ears to hear and eyes to see.

Lilly Blue, a teacher particularly concerned with facilitating children's capacity to write poetry, points out that "poetry is more than linguistic devices and distillations of sense and sound. In a world of visual bombardment and information-overwhelm, poetic encounters can provide responsive ways of seeing."[22] Blue identifies three elements which produce "fertile states" for creative hearing and seeing: "deep listening, meaningful silence, and acute attention." While Blue is specifically considering children as writers, her emphasis is relevant for readers of poetry as well, as she notes it is "deep reflective listening that can reveal epiphany or inspiration . . . in ways that are deeply impacting and transformative."[23] She comments that there are different qualities of silence that can be introduced into a room.

20. Ware, *Art of Prayer*, 110.

21. Kavanagh, *Collected Poems*, from the poem, "The Great Hunger."

22. Blue, "Poetry as a Way of Seeing," 26.

23. Blue, "Poetry as a Way of Seeing," 28.

Imposed silence in a classroom, she says, is very different from a creative silence where students are encouraged into a state of deep listening. At this point, "It is as if the floor of the room sinks and walls fall away, inviting the world to be heard differently."[24] One could wish that such creative silences would be introduced into religious studies classrooms and, indeed, into our own forms of worship.

The creative silence introduced into a classroom poetry workshop is very different from the silence a fisherman exudes sitting at the end of a pier, or that of a woman breastfeeding her newborn, or in the presence of angelic beings in silent worship. Each one carries a context, a quality, each its own texture and evocative capacity, its own shape and color. This is just as every door for every house differs. It may be hand-carved, or a commonly manufactured door that at first glance seems uninteresting and unremarkable. Yet each door leads to somewhere, just as each portal of silence leads to a place. Each door holds the question Jesus implies: Will you knock? (Matt 7:7–8). Or could it be that God is nudging us about our tiny door, calling us to "Behold, I stand at the door and knock" (Rev 3:20)?[25]

Silence and Music: Two Wings of Presence

Silence has long been an appropriate response to the Divine. Ephraim the Syrian, the great hymnologist and choir master of the fourth century, is attributed with the saying that silence is the language of the kingdom of heaven. Ephraim sees silence and music as inextricably woven together. And even the angelic beings in Revelation 8 are silent in awe and worship as the whole heavenly company responds to the opening of the scrolls with silent awe. The Dead Sea scrolls show how the early communities included silence in their worship, with the Songs of the Sabbath Sacrifice (otherwise known as the Angelic Liturgy) praising God with silence; and there are also references to the sound of blessing and the sound of quiet stillness.[26]

The contemporary Irish musician and poet Noirin Ni Riain coined the word "theosony" to refer to the theology of listening for God in sounds and silences. Her contention is that "listening, speaking, conversation, clairaudience and silence" have been largely neglected in theological discourse.[27] She suggests that "the realm of silence is a theological listening and, in turn, an

---

24. Blue, "Poetry as a Way of Seeing," 28.

25. *New American Standard Bible.*

26. Alexander, *Mystical Texts.*

27. Ni Riain, *Theosony,* 31.

answering to the sound of God."[28] She points out that the word "symphony" refers to the pairing of two notes, and so posits that God communicates in symphony through the two notes of silence and sound.

John Cage's silent composition entitled 4'33, in which the pianist simply sits at the piano not touching a note for four minutes and thirty-three seconds, was first performed in 1952. One of the purposes of this piece was for an audience to notice just how much sound there was in "silence"—the coughing, shuffling, and movements of people; the vibrations from distant traffic, and even the sounds unique to the building itself. Some composers deliberately employ silence as integral parts of their composition, and when we listen for these, each one carries its own contextualized message, and an opportunity to enter into that particular moment of stillness and silence. Of course, we can be listening to a deafening piece of music, and access the stillness and silence within ourselves and encounter God there. But in a world where there seems to be a great scarcity of silence and stillness, our focus here is more on identifying where silences external to us *can* be found, and harnessed into a contemplative practice.

When we listen to a piece of music, it can be easy to be unaware of the role silences are playing, and miss the invitations these may be issuing us. Listening to music, not just as a backdrop to whatever else we may be doing, but rather with an intentional focus, can enable us to soar on the two wings of silence and music together. As noted already, silence interplays with the notes and vice versa. The aviator-cum-author Ann Morrow Lindbergh wrote: "A note of music gains significance from the silence on either side."[29] One can imagine her in 1930 with her well-earned glider pilot's license (the first woman to qualify) taking to the air, hitching a ride on a thermal, and gliding on hours of delicious silence over wide spans and wingspans of horizons and landscapes. I wonder what significance her gliding silences gave to the musical undertones of her life that sat between these skied silences. Perhaps it enabled her to recognize her own truths: "The most exhausting thing in life, I have discovered, is being insincere. That is why so much of social life is exhausting; one is wearing a mask. I have shed my mask. . . . Women need solitude in order to find again the true essence of themselves."[30]

Music holds a space for silence, and enables us to lift silence up to our lips and drink it. Elena Katz-Chernin revealed in an interview in 2018 how she changed her music when her son of fourteen was diagnosed with

---

28. Ni Riain, *Theosony*, 185.

29. Lindbergh, *Gift from the Sea*, 42.

30. Lindbergh, *Gift from the Sea*, 55.

schizophrenia.[31] His longing to hear silence in the midst of the noise and voices in his head guided Elena as she composed her music. One piece, specifically for her son and others who have similar struggles, she called *Blue Silence*. It is a string quartet that holds silence cupped in its phrasing; sensitive and beckoning it holds its liquid silence up to be sipped. It is a piece of music for many of us who find we have too much noise in our busy heads, and desire the elixir of silence.

31. Katz-Chernin, "Blue Silence."

6

Ma: Emptiness Full of Possibility

MA
Thirty spokes meet in the hub,
though the space between them is the essence of the wheel.
Pots are formed from clay,
though the space inside them is the essence of the pot.
Walls with windows and doors form the house,
though the space within them is the essence of the house.[1]

Ma is an aesthetic value found in many realms of Japanese life and culture. The traditional Japanese poem above alludes to the way spaces are an intrinsic part of the whole. Examples include the spaces created in an Ikebana arrangement, the space within and around calligraphy or other traditional art forms, the spaces between rocks in a Japanese garden made in a dry riverbed; in the shaping of windows, verandas, and other aspects of Japanese architecture. Whatever culture or country we are in, we encounter many visual open spaces every day, often without noticing them. The

1. Traditional Japanese poem, https://wawaza.com/blogs/when-less-is-more-japan ese-concept-of-ma-minimalism-and-beyond/.

so-called negative spaces in a painting, the open spaces between doorposts or even between the branches of a tree, and the carefully arranged objects within a garden all positioned around a space are all forms of *ma*.

It is also an intrinsic part of conversation in Japanese culture where, contrary to Western conversation styles, it is not deemed necessary to spell everything out or fill every silence, but rather allow *ma*, to allow space, silence, stillness to speak. And when a youngster is taught to bow, at the deep point of the bow, they are instructed to pause, to *ma*, in order for the bow to be both given and received well. While in Western culture, *ma* may often be seen as nothing, or blank space, in Japanese culture it has a rich heritage and meaning. *Ma* is written as 間, where the character 門 depicts a door or gateway, with either the sun 日 or the moon 月 portrayed inside the door peeping through the opening. Onlookers are invited to move forward into the *ma* themselves, not only to peer through like the sun or the moon, but to enter in fully.

I had the opportunity to spend two years overseas as part of a sabbatical, in a small town not far from Chicago. It was in that context I came to explore the wonder of *ma* in two very different places. The first was in among some ordinary trees planted just near our apartment. And the second was in the detailed painting process of a twelfth-century icon while on retreat in New Mexico's high desert. In both cases, I found myself being drawn to those apparently blank, vacuous, and sometimes threatening chasms, and discovering *ma* to be a wise guide offering me new ways to pray.

MA IN OUR MIDST

Ma within Nature

Since arriving in this new country, I had come to befriend a tree that became an "Aslan" presence for me. I had watched this tree from our apartment window and, as it rocked in the breezes, the branches seemed to move in large clumps, like the clumps of hair on a great St. Bernard dog, or like that of a lion loping with its thick mane moving in rhythm. I had been feeling disorientated, in an interstice between the home that I had left, and this new place that wasn't yet home. I have long enjoyed C. S. Lewis's Narnia series, where he portrayed God as a great lion called Aslan.[2] The tree evoked for me something of Aslan, and so I pulled the Narnia books out again, and a quote stood out for me: "Wrong will be right, when Aslan comes in sight, / At the sound of his roar, sorrows will be no more, / When he bares his teeth,

2. Lewis, *Lion, the Witch and the Wardrobe.*

winter meets its death, / And when he shakes his mane, we shall have spring again."[3] "When he shakes his mane." This was indeed an Aslan tree, calling me to come near and take shelter.

At first it looked like a single large evergreen fir tree, but when I went for the first time to stand under it, I discovered there were in fact two trees, close together, so close that they had seemed to merge as one tree. There, I found myself under the arch of Aslan with the trees being the back and front legs. And there was even a stump between them where I could sit. How could this be? This was a chapel of space bridged by the body of God. I was enveloped under the great fur of the belly of God, with the mane gently moving with the wind.

Over a period of weeks and then months, it came to be the space where I would pray, a sacred place both in sun and snow where I felt my identity became wrapped in God's great mane of care and comfort.

One evening I wandered there under the great branches, under the hearth and heart of Aslan. It had been a particularly difficult time. I had felt squeezed and compressed by some pressures and fearful situations that were piling one on top of the other. I had been praying desperately over a period of months regarding a particular circumstance, and yet each morning when I woke, things seemed to progressively deteriorate. The more I prayed, the worse things seemed to get. I felt bereft of God's presence, abandoned and stranded in a place within myself that I had begun to call "Nowhere." I took this Nowhere with me under the tree and sat, tissue-thin in my sense of self.

It was a day when the temperatures had plummeted; it was dry, and the sun had broken through, now low in the evening sky. Snow caked the branches and all was still. There was a penumbral depth of silence. I started noticing the spaces between the branches, the blank places where there was no branch, no fir needles, as if these were the lacunae where there was no God—the hiatus of no presence—yet swirling threateningly like hungry, insatiable black holes. They began to grow and become like chasms, great yawning gaps resonating with the rifts within my soul. Some sunlight reached through the gaps, but it only made the spaces more untouchable, too harsh with shiny-bright whiteness, and I turned my eyes away.

I had been reaching, yearning, grasping at the edges of God's garment, like the woman with the flow of blood (Luke 8:43–48). Yet she had touched something, tugged at it with gritty determination, and came away with a whole surprising handful and a new cloak of healed belonging. Yet I was coming adrift, unable to grasp the mane, sliding down a slippery slope and beginning to be swallowed up as though by a polar vortex in a place

3. Lewis, *Lion, the Witch and the Wardrobe*, 74–75.

called Nowhere, spinning out of control, any warmth turning into dead, cold stiffness.

The wind blew lightly. I became aware of some of the snow being caught up—it was so cold and dry that the snow seemed to splinter off the branches into ice sparks that were carried in the breeze. In the midst of my own freeze, I was captivated by the beauty around me. Tiny shards of light were carried on the breath of wind, glinting in the sunlight, sparkling and airborne. Aslan's mane billowed gently, and the wind through the pine needles took on a soothing murmuring of companionship. Was that Aslan humming? I looked again at gaps and breaks between branches. I began to see that the beauty and shape of the tree was made up by the shapes of these spaces between limbs that made the whole. The gaps between branches—those apparent "nothingnesses"—were maybe, just maybe, quite the opposite: perhaps they were full. Maybe, just maybe, these were holding spaces, silken and smooth like soft wombs of air holding embryonic possibilities. As I twisted around to look at all the spaces above me, I shifted my feet, and became aware of the soft, spongy soil underneath. There was such a thick carpet of fallen needles under the snow, and slowly it seemed I was touching the soft felted texture of a pelt. I was being cocooned in a pelted pouch between the earth and the tree, a pouch under Aslan, tucked into the belly of God.

I began to recall the Japanese concept of *ma* that I had been researching. I looked again—now with a sacred seeing—at the spaces between structures of branches and saw *ma*. These were not neglected gaps but rather beautiful shapes and patterns, with their own gift, their own message. And of course, silences between words and statements speak their own sentenced language. Perhaps too, I began to think, silences between God-Presences could hold great weight and significance—a dark and heavy weight sometimes, yet nevertheless such darkness may be held on either side by light, secured in place by pillars of Presence. Just like the legs of Aslan forming this fir tree chapel. Perhaps I no longer needed to fear the gaps, the fissures, and chasms. They are part of my life, and come and go with changing seasons, just like the interstices between all trees' branches which change with the seasons. Sometimes they feel emptier and darker and more vacuous than other times. And maybe some of the huge pressures and squeezes that I have been experiencing are part of the birth pangs I have to endure.

I was now extremely cold, but I was feeling a tiny rising of hope. My wispy self seemed to be gathering itself into a more solid bundle of possibilities. I began to amble back to our warm apartment, crunching across the snow. What I had seen and come to touch and be touched by could become a gateway forward, I thought, a gate—a *ma*—with pillars of God on either side. Or a soft, slippery birth tunnel, ushering me out into the felted pouch of a newborn. *Ma* had been dwelling in the gaps. God, appearing to be silent and distant, had opened a way by which I could move forward into the days ahead. Maybe wrong *would* eventually be made right, when Aslan comes loping, shaking his mane, and spring *will* at last come again.

Ma within Icons

Some months later, I was needing a break from study, and longing for space and silence. I had been scrolling through possible retreats being advertised, and one leapt off the page: an iconography retreat, outside Santa Fe. I had done some iconography before, and found it to be process that absorbed me into prayerfulness. Half an hour later, I had booked my place and my flights. And before I knew it, I was arriving at the retreat center late one evening.

The first morning I awoke before dawn, eager to explore. The early morning air was sharp, and the light just touching the sky as I made way up onto the small mesa behind my cabin to watch the sunrise here in the high desert of New Mexico. Slung between the Colorado Basin and the Rio Grande rift, this ancient landscape was formed more than two hundred million years ago. Everywhere I looked, as the early sunlight crept down the mountains and escarpments, the light picked out first the tops of grey mudstone, followed by the yellow and white quartz sandstone layers, changing to pink and then below that to dark maroon shales, landing in the valley with red siltstones of the arroyo below me. This earthy pigment light show seemed such an appropriate way to begin a day of icon writing, where I would be using the natural pigments of the land mixed into an egg tempera paint in the ancient practice of iconography.

I had come for a week, joining a small group of others in this spacious and silent landscape to learn more about the deeply spiritual practice of iconography and together each writing the twelfth-century icon, *Vladimir Mother of God*, or *Theotokos* (God-bearer). Icons are referred to as something that is written rather than painted, as iconography is much more a form of prayer than it is a form of art. In the Orthodox Christian tradition, this icon is known as being of the *eleusa* or *umileniye* type, meaning tenderness, pathos, and loving-kindness. Our guide reminded us throughout the process to be continually praying the Jesus prayer in rhythm with our breathing, "Lord Jesus Christ, Son of God, have mercy on me."

Standing by our tables to begin, we prayed together the "Iconographer's Prayer," praying this each time we arrived at the table to pick up our brushes and paint. "O Divine Lord of all that exists," it begins. "Enlighten my soul, my heart, and my spirit. . . . Grant me also the desire, the will, and the gift of Thy grace, that my own distorted image may be transfigured into thy Divine Likeness. . . . Thou hast said, 'Without Me ye can do nothing.' O my Lord, with faith I embrace Thy words and bow down before Thy goodness." An ancient prayer, with the form of language reminding me that this venerable practice came from a big canvas, encompassing cultures, peoples, and faiths about which I knew very little. I felt I was descending into one of the desert canyons, except instead of dropping down past layer upon layer of Mesozoic rock, I was being lowered down through layers of time into the communion of saints.

The whole painting process was like a prayer itself. The final sanding of the gesso was left for each of us to do after our iconography instructor had prepared the wooden boards already with five layers of gesso. The gentle, rhythmic sanding helped us get to know the wood and its surface, and evoked in me the work of the Holy Spirit, who sometimes used friction in my life to sand back my sharp edges. And so, I found myself praying that bit by bit I might have fewer abrasive edges, and become to the touch as this silken smooth texture that the gesso board was now taking on. This apparently blank space was rich with texture. Ah, I thought, here is *ma*, greeting me from this white satiny surface, bounded only by the edges of the board. An empty space of board, filled with possibility. *Ma*—this is my friend, a teacher surprising me with its presence. This time not from between branches, but held in my hands. I couldn't help running my hands over and over the surface. So satin-smooth. Like the Christ-child's face we would be sketching on the gessoed surface. I imagined I could feel his cheek as I held it in my mother-hands.

After sketching the Mother and the Christ-child, the first element to bring to the board was gold leaf. It was the perfect weather for it: dry and still. If there is high humidity, or there are cross breezes, it makes the handling of gold leaf too difficult. After painting on the gold size (special glue), it was time to place the fragile, luminous gold leaf. When I held one of the squares of gold leaf up to the light with special tweezers, it was so fine I could see through it. It was so delicate that it couldn't touch my fingers or it would break and stick to my skin. I felt apprehensive—this can so easily go wrong, I thought, and this precious, twenty-four-carat gold could end up all over the place, except where it needed to be.

In iconography, gold represents divinity and light. It was an amazing thought to be holding these symbolic fragments of divinity and light in my hands. I felt a deep awe as I consciously opened my heart into surrender. I took my time. I could feel the change within me as my body, which had been tense with concerns about "messing it up," began to relax into the hands of the Divine Artist who would guide and direct. I took up a sheet of the gold leaf from the pad and then, with gentle blowing and lowering, the gold found its way onto the glue-sheened gesso. Piece by piece, breath by breath, the gold began to cover the area of Jesus and Mary's halos, as well as the background. It was like uniting with the Spirit, with *Ruach*, breath with Breath, breathing together as one as divinity and light found its way onto the silken surface softly and soundlessly. My hands were being guided, my breathing partnered, my presence suffused with Presence. All of us in the room were bent into the moment of concentration, the air so still.

After a walk in the freshness outside and relaxing from the intense focus, it was time to begin the slow burnishing of the gold. I wandered back into our painting room early, and no one else was in the room. Strangely, this didn't make the room feel empty, but rather I experienced it as filled with the presence of relationships: the careful placing of each table with its own icon working space for each person near a window for natural light. The deliberate neat setting out of the pigments, brushes, and gold leaf pads. And still hanging in the air, almost suspended with anticipation, all the gentle breaths that had guided the golf leaf seemed to linger. What was this room of *ma* saying to me? What was its message? I too lingered in the doorway. It seemed the space was alive with breath—our breath and the breathing of God, and I began to breathe in as deeply as I could, wanting to fill myself with this breath of Life. To breathe in God and breathe out God. But I couldn't breathe in enough, I had an insatiable desire to be filled to the fullness of this breathing God. Behind me, I heard the sound of footsteps approaching along the dusty path, and I took one long, last breath. *Ma* was guiding me into the Spirit's presence.

We gathered again under the watchful eyes of our iconographer guide. We each had a smooth agate stone, which we used with circular movements of light pressure, to press out the creases, joins, and crinkles of the gold leaf. I was polishing the halo of God! And smoothing the golden light all around Mary and Christ, burnishing and bowing to this luminous Light. My body knew instinctively how to respond, as I continued to bow like the *ma* bow, honoring deeply this Christ-Light. As I burnished, my hands felt guided in knowing how much to do, the level of pressure that was right, the circular movements that would enhance and not break the gold-leaf-light. And the tiny scraps of gold left over were like divinity littering the rest of the board and the table. A generosity and extravagance scattering the seed of gold everywhere, as if to say, "Do not worry: there is divinity to spare, more than enough for all and for everywhere." The Christ-child had welcomed me into this golden circle with his Mother, into the embrace of this lightly sketched silence of intimate embrace.

Next was the making of the tempera medium to mix with the pigments. Our guide gave us each some farm-fresh eggs. They need to be fresh or the membrane around the yoke can be too weak to work with. The room was filled with a hushed concentration. The crackings of eggshells on the sides of the bowls fractured the air with their chalky-white sounds. It was a reminder to me of both the beauty and fragility of life. I let the sticky egg white flow into the bowl, passing the yoke from one half-shell to the other. Once most of the white has run off, we were to hold the egg yolk in our hands and, again, roll it from one cupped hand to the other, allowing the yolk to become drier. Soft, smooth, precious like a baby's creamy fine-velvet skin. What treasure, to hold an egg yolk and not have the liquid simply drip away through my fingers. We then held the yolk in one hand between our fingers, and gently punctured the membrane with a spatula, letting the yellow pour into a cup and holding the membrane back. A rupturing of membranes like the breaking of membranes in childbirth. And iconography for me was becoming like a labor: a labor of love, of birthing an icon, and of newness being birthed within myself.

A drop of white vinegar was then added to our yolk to help preserve the mixture from forming mold, and then drops of water were added and stirred in until the right consistency was reached. Taking a very small scoop of pigment—which was so fine we had to wear a mask as the particles can become airborne so easily—we mixed this into the medium to form a smooth, rich texture. I gazed into my cup. Not a cup to drink, but a cup to worship with when I would place this paint on the board, on the skin of Jesus and Mary.

We painted mostly in silence over the next several days, layer upon layer of paint, layer upon layer of silence. In this tradition it is understood that the paint is received by the board, just as we were to be receptive to God's movements in us. As we painted, we were encouraged to become one in prayer with the painting, the brush, and the guiding hand of the Spirit. Just as the board received the paint with a surrendered-ness, *Gelassenheit*—the tranquil submission that the mystics speak of in the Presence of the Divine—so too my spirit was to become surrendered to this gentle Artist-Spirit.

The first layering of paint was the base layer for the face and hands. I had done a number of icons by now, but it came again as a surprise just how strange this first color on the skin is. The *proplasmos* method has the first layer as a combination of yellow ochre and raw umber, forming an olive green. The faces and skin are painted with this greenish color that feels so strange and unredeemable. This requires two coats, as if in reply to the disbelief that this color could possibly be correct. It has a translucency and covers all hair, hands, skin, and faces. It is meant to reflect the color of clay, a reminder of the clay from which all flesh is formed. Before me was the beginning of the incarnation emerging from the gesso. Earth pigments forming clay color, combined with egg yolk—a symbol of new life—was to touch this incarnating God before me, arising in such a real and earthy way. The texture of presence, not clear yet, was still a wash of wet clay, with features yet to emerge.

Then slowly the first highlight was brushed on, using a combination of yellow ochre with white and a drop of red oxide. In iconography, yellow represents the light of God, with white as purity or the Holy Spirit and red oxide as earth, humanity, and the blood of sacrifice. Light, Spirit, and blood, a confronting combination of colors. And already the traces of sacrifice— both that of Jesus and of Mary—were emerging all too quickly. I wanted to push back that streak of blood in the paint. This felt too early, too soon, too violating of the newness and freshness of emerging life. Trauma and violation embedded in their bodies, reflect mine, reflect theirs. The icon functions also as a mirror, picking up my own streaks and crevasses etched too deep for words. Yet here was a held place before me, the Mother and Child who have gone before me into all the red oxides of experience. My body cried out, "No." I cried out, "No." I sat for a long time before I could begin to say yes to the paint, yes to the cross, yes to God.

I spent that evening playing in the dirt just as I had in my childhood, with a cup of water and some clay down in the gully nearby, and I let God speak to me through the clay in my hands. My own clay body formed by God—every detail, every layer of me had been gently molded into existence. And God, too, had come as clay to me that day, touching me through Jesus and his Mother, the *Theotokos*, the God-bearer holding God in her arms. The texture and smell of clay lingered on my skin into the night. Did it linger on God's hands too?

The next day we painted layers for the face, with a total of seven layers making up the face, each layer covering less and less of the skin, and each shade being lighter and lighter. Seven: the number representing completion, and the number of days I was spending on this retreat. I continued with more yellow-with-white, then red oxide and a clear medium. The clear felt like it represented water, mixing with the color of blood—the birthing fluids that flowed from Mary as she birthed Jesus, and that also flowed from the side of Christ on the cross as he birthed the church. How can I make way for this birthing God to speak to me even through this small icon coming to life in my hands?

Burnt umber—the color of poverty and monastic life—traced the eyebrows and irises. I gazed for a long time into the eyes of Mary and Jesus.

How did they see the world through eyes of poverty? And burnt sienna, another color of poverty, tracing the noses, lips, eyelids, ears, and fingers. Suddenly it occurred to me, these are the senses: smell, taste, sight, sound, touch—all outlined in "poverty." When Jesus became a person, he also took on with his deity all our senses and all our poverty too. And here in front of me was the juxtaposition of the gold of divinity, the earthy clay of humanity and incarnation outlined in poverty. This was a paradoxical God, both God and human at once. The icon was holding the paradox, expressing the inexpressible: the One who is beyond expression yet here emerging as an image; the infinite uncreated One depicted using created finite materials of the earth; the intangible presented through the tangible; the invisible through the visible. Here was my theology of incarnation, of God-come-close.

Over the last days, the layers of color filled out the clothes, and the transparency of each underlying color showed through each thin float of paint. Then came the finishing off with a linseed oil varnish, made from crushing the seeds to extract the goodness. The lives of Christ and of Mary were subject to crushing suffering, and from this such goodness of resurrection flowed from God's paintbrush in big, broad strokes.

I was continually drawn to gazing on what seemed like the vast space of blank gold in the icon as I was completing it. I took the icon, still damp and fresh, across the room to place it under a window to look more closely. When I laid it down, I realized I had placed my thumb right at the center of the top, leaving a thumb-shaped smudge on the layered gold leaf! My first response was a mix of horror and disappointment. But no, this is the freedom of an icon: I give myself to the process of creating it, and then allow whatever it is to be my prayer offering to God. This was not about achievement or perfection, I reminded myself, but simply about prayer. It was as if this very smudge was to rub out of me any sense of getting caught up in anxiety or pride about what I had produced, and spun me back to the truth that this was simply about my offering of being present to God. I came on this retreat to pray with the process of iconography, not to produce a work of art. I grinned at the smudge, and welcomed its message. And what was more, my thumb, my own body, had entered into the golden *ma*. I wondered: isn't that in fact what I am called toward—to place my very self into the expansively rich *ma* space of God—that part of God which goes beyond definitions and particulars?

It was to the encounters with the God of *ma* that I returned time and again: the sheer white of the gessoed board before we started; the response of my body with a *ma* bow as I burnished; the *ma* of the room in which we gathered to do our work; and the negative space on the icon of the plain gold area that held no particular features.

This gold part of the icon felt extensive, and at first almost unnecessary, as I was eager to move my gaze on to the tender faces of Mary and Jesus. I had found myself wondering: yes, it is the two halos and their surrounds, but why so extensive? I was drawn back again to this spaciousness of gold, this nothing space, this *ma* space. And as I felt drawn into it, I began to feel it as the ground of heavenly light, which had the function of focusing and making the figures "pop out" of the icon. Even as I was working on it, the icon was becoming a window into this intimate embrace between Mother and Child. And the window was open, the gold space became the whole realm of heaven and earth holding out in this frame a story of pathos and tenderness so exquisite as to be inexpressible. My attention kept moving to the *ma* gold space, then back to their faces; to the *ma* and back to their eyes; the gold space and back to the hand of Jesus; the *ma* and back to their pressed cheeks. It was as if the gold space of *ma* kept on illuminating and identifying certain aspects of their deep cherishing, the tender knowing that held all the suffering and piercing of hearts that was to come. This was the mystical soft inner light, the uncreated light of God radiating outwards. The past, present, and future were shimmering in this one moment.

That night I slept out on the cooling evening clay-dust under the stars. I took my time and bowed low and long, *ma*-like, before the huge desert sky, before the God who is Infinite Tender Love. The love that had enveloped me as I meditated through the icon was now drawing out of me a love toward God that was saturating, drenching me in a tempera of warmth and gratitude, yoking me with an ache to this beautiful and boundless God. Under the sky seemed the only fitting place to be; the presence of the One who breathed and shone through time and space was too big. Too big for me to go to sleep between four walls in a small roofed room. I needed to touch the sky with this expansive God and with all of my being. I was touching into and being touched by the company of the Trinity who reaches through small gold blank spaces of *ma*, of apparent nothingness, and draws me— even me—into their tender embrace together.

REFLECTION

The Shape of Trees

I had previously researched the etymology of the word "contemplation": *con*, meaning "with," or "together"; and *templum*, meaning "an open place, a sanctuary, a temple, a place of presence."[4] This *templum* is similar to *ma* and can represent open sacred spaces, including those within each person and between persons, within me and between myself and others, a sacred space where I could easily assume nothing is there, that nothing is happening. When the gap in the trees took on the aesthetic value of *ma*, what had begun as an external reflection of my interior experience—a vacuous chasm of nothingness—became instead not a thing on its own, but an integral part of the whole. The branches held the spaces. The gaps were not done away with, just as painful encounters with profound darkness are not extracted from my experiences, but rather part of a bigger whole: a whole in which the Divine is fully involved.

Constance Fitzgerald, a discalced Carmelite and contemporary contemplative theologian, explains what may be happening when we experience the gaps or chasms that come to us. She gave this address at a young novice's first profession—sure counsel for the beginning of a long journey. Referencing John of the Cross, she suggests that during such times,

> We are being radically opened to encounter the God who is beyond the limits of our expectations, beyond our constrained imaginings, not defined by our memories or held by our boundaries. We are brought to silence so that we might truly hope, brought to emptiness so that we might be filled, so that we might transcend our very selves. This is why the contemplative life moves into vision and the liminal experience of prophetic imagination, as the mystics know. . . . Today our visions and locutions are the witness we make from living on the edge of the horizon. "Vision" for us is seeing over the horizon; "locutions" are hearing the call forward, for ourselves and others, into the new consciousness that awaits us there, into new ways of being and seeing.[5]

Our horizons can be very close to us. It can be impossible to see beyond the horizon of the chasm that engulfs us, enclosing us in a void. Yet a horizon doesn't exist as a thing in and of itself. It is not a rigid boundary line at which we can stand, but rather moves with us, and is related to where we are in the world, and where we are looking. *Ma* invites me to shift position, see horizons and spaces differently. Fitzgerald reminds us there is a beyond-ness that we are invited to see and a call to hear that slowly may help us become boundary-crossers and horizon-shifters as we traverse our interior landscapes.

4. Longley, "Patience and the Act of Nurturing."
5. Fitzgerald, "Carmelite Beatitudes," no page number.

Fitzgerald is not advocating a quick fix. The processes by which we are "brought to silence" and "brought to emptiness" are terrible. Gerard Manley Hopkins (1844–89), a Jesuit priest and English poet, helps us not shy away from the reality of the chasms that lie below the cliff edge, when he writes what is known as his "terrible sonnets." And Psalm 88 is another example of not turning away from the reality of the dark night of the soul. Unlike the majority of psalms, instead of finishing on an upward and hope-filled note, the psalmist lands at the bottom of the cliff with, "And darkness is my only friend."

The experience I had of being held in the pouch of God—a motherly image—evokes a well-known Scripture passage, but one that mostly has not been translated well. The prologue of John's Gospel, profoundly mystical in nature, refers to *kolpos*, meaning fold of a garment, bosom, lap, womb, or heart. Stramara suggests the verse may be translated as, "No one has ever seen God except the only Son who came to lead us to the womb (*kolpos*) of the Father" (John 1:18).[6] He points out that to many it would seem that "the very idea of the 'womb of the Father' is so jarring that it appears totally ludicrous."[7] He goes on to argue the validity of such an interpretation, setting his understanding within the context of the whole of John's Gospel, which embraces new birth as a central concept. Further, Stramara draws on early church fathers, such as Clement of Alexandria (150–215 CE) and Athanasius of Alexandria (296–373 CE), demonstrating that as early as the third century there was an understanding of John 1:18 referring to the "womb of the Father." The *kolpos* is generative in nature, a place where new possibilities are conceived in love. Wombs and pouches offer safe containers when we are helpless, and here we are nourished, to emerge with new beginnings and new skin, as silky as God.

The day under the Aslan tree had come after some weeks of deep despair. This movement, ignited by the sparks of ice splinters glistening aloft on the breeze, was a long time coming. Yet when it did, it seemed to rush forward into a unity of which John speaks. In John 17 Jesus prays that we will be one with Jesus and Abba, just as Jesus is in Abba and Abba is in Jesus. This is an intimacy that is a mystery. Being brought into the womb or pouch of God are times of great vulnerability, yet it is in such times of utter dependence that the mysterious gift is given, of the mortal becoming one with the Divine. Still clawing at empty air, sometimes we can find ourselves mysteriously held.

6. Stramara, "Kolpos," 37.
7. Stramara, "Kolpos," 27.

Being Guided by Icons and Iconography

An icon occupies the borderland between the visible and the invisible. It offers a window, not to be worshiped itself, but to frame ways of seeing that offer new vistas. It seems to bring together the paradox of God being both immanent and transcendent. Russian-born iconographers Ouspensky and Lossky describe the dilemma, "Both theology and iconography are faced with a problem which is absolutely insoluble—to express by means belonging to the created world that which is infinitely above the creature."[8] There is always the tension, the gap that exists between immortal, ineffable, and immaterial Reality and what we are capable of expressing. Yet we have two lenses: the *ma* lens of Japan and the icon lens of Orthodoxy. There seemed to me to be a conversation happening between these two lenses. The Orthodox lens offered a window through the tangible icon into the intangible wonder of an omnipresent God. And the *ma* lens invited me to enter fully with my whole being into this expansive gold leaf area giving off ineffable light. Both lenses when brought together offered two different yet overlapping perspectives and so, like stereoscopic vision, formed a view of different dimensions which enabled a clearer spiritual sight, a way into mystery.

Choosing to create an icon over a period of days in the midst of a desert landscape afforded me the opportunity to go deep into the process. Very little was said by the instructor, just what was essential, and he left the rest up to our own discovery and prayer as we entered this divine milieu. The icon offers us an image through which to begin praying, and then prayer is often transported into an imageless presencing in the Divine. Diarmaid MacCulloch, a specialist in ecclesiastical history, refers to the wisdom of Francis de Sales, a bishop and mystic writing in the 1600s, who suggested that meditation (kataphatic prayer using images and words) and contemplation (apophatic prayer which is imageless and wordless) "can flow in and out of each other."[9]

There are no shadows in icons. Traditional Western art starts with light paint and progressively adds dark. As we behold an icon, the light embodied in it is portrayed as radiating from within the icon as the uncreated Light. Over the process, I began to see how a luminosity seemed to be emanating from the incomplete icon as if Genesis was climbing out of its cracked eggshell and poking through into the small scene before me.

It had been explained to me that the symbolism of a very large egg that we saw hanging near the iconostasis in an Egyptian Coptic church refers

8. Ouspensky and Lossky, *Meaning of Icons*, 49.

9. MacCulloch, *Silence*, 82.

to the fact that mother ostriches focus on their egg and rarely take their eyes from it until the egg hatches. This is intended as a visible and symbolic reminder to all who see it, that God the Mother never takes her eyes off us, and we are to forever fix our eyes on God, the one who births us. Together, the egg tempera I was working with and the symbology of the ostrich egg seem now to wrap me in the safe membrane of a compassionate and watching Mother God.

The palette of colors used is with intentional reference to the original icon and to the traditional associations each color has. The contemporary American iconographer Christine Hales describes her own journey with egg tempera.

> There's a way that light travels between the layers and comes back to the eye that is infinitely more pleasing than an acrylic flat color comprised of a mixture of the same colors. It is a different aesthetic experience that registers within the soul. It is something like the difference between polyester and linen. Both can be the same color, but have a different feel and appearance.[10]

The theology of icons speaks through the colors, lines, and shapes of the icon. In this way, the icon speaks in the silence, guides, and sheds light on our own souls with a texture that is luminous and illuminating.

It was the space of *ma* in the icon that became my focus. This expansively small space encircling the faces of Jesus and Mary, filled with gold, brimming with possibility. Hales speaks of the so-called background of icons as "creating a uniform and infinite space. It becomes a container for everything."[11] When I made the thumb smudge on the golden *ma*, it gave me a gift: it revealed to me the fear I had been carrying underneath the surface, and freed me to live lightly in the process. A reminder, again, that iconography is not for admiration of the artistic elements, and that they are not intended for aesthetic admiration. It is a form of living art, offering inspiration for prayer and contemplation.

This was one of my key learnings. It was the smudged gold *ma* that was teaching me some deep lessons. If a mistake is made with paint it can be fixed. If a mistake is made with the gold leaf, it stays. This gold area was the *ma* of the icon: that place that I had assumed to be blank, empty space—yes, gold, but nevertheless vacant and of less meaning than the rest. Yet this was the locus, the place, the space to which was I was continually drawn back, and eventually by mistake placed my own body in it, and received a gift.

10. Hales, *Eyes of Fire*, ch. 7, para. 25, Kindle location 2015.

11. Hales, *Eyes of Fire*, Appendix A, para. 4.

PONDERING YOUR OWN EXPERIENCES

- "I started noticing the spaces between the branches, the blank places where there was no branch, no fir needles, as if these were the lacunae where there was no God—the hiatus of no presence. They began to grow and become like chasms, great yawning gaps resonating with the rifts within my soul." Sometimes what is in the external landscape can reflect back to us our internal landscapes. What are some of the *ma* spaces around you in your external landscape, and what are they reflecting back to you?

- "The gaps between branches—those apparent 'nothingnesses'—were maybe, just maybe, quite the opposite: perhaps they were full." Perhaps you or a loved one is experiencing the pain of "nothingness" in some form or other. What might be some ways forward?

- From the ancient iconographer's prayer, these words may be something you would like to mediate on: "Enlighten my soul, my heart, and my spirit. . . . Grant me also the desire, the will, and the gift of Thy grace, that my own distorted image may be transfigured into thy Divine Likeness. . . . Thou hast said, 'Without Me ye can do nothing.'"

- "Already the traces of sacrifice—both that of Jesus and of Mary—were emerging all too quickly. I wanted to push back that streak of blood in the paint. This felt too early, too soon, too violating of the newness and freshness of emerging life." What experiences in your own life does this evoke within you? How do you hold such an experience?

- "Just as the board received the paint with a surrendered-ness, *Gelassenheit*—the tranquil submission that the mystics speak of in the Presence of the Divine—so too my spirit was to become surrendered to this gentle Artist-Spirit." The white gessoed board to begin with held expansive *ma* space. And then the gold that embraced the figures of Mother and Child offered a deep sense of *ma* to enter into. It can feel all too vulnerable to choose a surrendered-ness which allows us to enter the spaces of apparent nothingness. We more often want to be in control. What can you do to help yourself move toward a tranquil submission as you enter prayer?

- You may wish to refer to a photograph of the twelfth-century icon that has been mentioned, *Our Lady of Vladimir* or *Theotokos*, currently hanging in the Hall Museum Church of St. Nicholas, Moscow.[12] The

12. https://en.wikipedia.org/wiki/Theotokos_of_Vladimir.

image offers the opportunity to meditate on the theologies of broken-ness, aging, worn-out-ness and our own historical journeys, and yet be able to see the beauty of God through the whole.

FOR FURTHER ENGAGEMENT

Ma in Culture and Conversation

When we have visited our Japanese friends, there is a sunken place just in-side their door, where we exchange our outside shoes for house slippers. This sunken space with its small boundary wall provides a physical *ma*—a structured place to pause, to enter fully into the hospitality being offered. The concept of *ma* includes a time element. Unlike the Western understand-ing of three-dimensional space being fixed, to which we add the fourth di-mension of time, *ma* is a dynamic spatial concept, where time is inextricably bound with space.[13]

Ma uses a physical open space to affect movement, adjusting the di-rection and speed in the way we move. In a Japanese strolling garden, the stepping stones are placed very specifically at certain intervals, with care-fully chosen *ma* between stones, to guide the speed with which we walk as well as the direction. And the traditional Japanese "Noh" theater puts great emphasis on the spaces between actors, the pace of movements of the actors and the spaces within speech. What becomes important is what the actor does *not* do or does *not* say. It is a rich concept. Art director and designer Alan Fletcher, expresses it well:

> Space is substance. Cézanne painted and modelled space. Giacometti sculpted by "taking the fat off space." Mallarmé con-ceived poems with absences as well as words. Ralph Richardson asserted that acting lay in pauses. . . . Isaac Stern described mu-sic as "that little bit between each note—silences which give the form." . . . The Japanese have a word (Ma) for this interval which gives shape to the whole. In the West we have neither word nor term. A serious omission.[14]

For a Westerner who needs to fill spaces, the amount of silence and stillness in the Noh drama—the *ma* moments—can be puzzling and dif-ficult to read.

13. Nitschke, "Ma—The Japanese Sense of Place."
14. Fletcher, *Art of Looking*, 294.

Yet *ma* is also within our own cultures and in Scripture, if we allow ourselves to become aware of them in a more intentional way. MacCulloch, in his detailed exploration of silence, *Silence: A Christian History*, documents many silences, including those within Scripture that could easily go unnoticed. Luke's Gospel in particular seems to be written with a sensitivity toward these silences. MacCulloch points these out, one of which is when "the Lord turned and looked at Peter" (Luke 22:61), stating that "it is one of the most eloquent stares in human history."[15] Hannah prays wordlessly and tearfully (1 Sam 1:13–16), and Jesus' own retreating into solitude has been a major focus in many commentaries, as has his silence when addressed by Pilate, and in the suffering servant passages. We all use and encounter such silences, such momentous *ma* moments, but with the fast pace of our lives, we may skim across these, rarely give them the attention and receptivity required to enable deep processing of their implications. MacCulloch quotes Clement of Alexandria (150–215 CE) that when we pray contemplatively, "we speak in silence."[16] So when we converse with the Divine, we may use the language of words or the language of silence.

Entering Ma Requires the Art of Patience

In order to be able to identify the many *ma* spaces all around us, to see them, and to be able to enter into their nuanced gifts to us, there is the need for us to develop a contemplative pace to our lives. And such a life requires patience to be at the heart of it.

Elif Shafak's comment helps us see patience as creative possibility rather than an end in itself. He suggests that "patience does not mean to passively endure. It means to be farsighted enough to trust the end result of a process. Patience is not sitting and waiting, it is foreseeing. It is looking at the thorn and seeing the rose, looking at the night and seeing the day."[17] This is a sacramental seeing that comes with a contemplative way of being in the world. It is looking at the gaps or negative spaces and seeing the fullness of presence.

Galatians 5:22 uses *makrothymia* (Greek) to refer to steadfastness and staying power, a patient and slow-to-anger stance. The Chinese character for patience points out that patience is far from easy, and requires the capacity for sustained attention even in the midst of what can be excruciating circumstances. Phonetically pronounced as "ren," it means patience, tolerance,

15. MacCulloch, *Silence*, 34.

16. MacCulloch, *Silence*, 62.

17. Shafak, *Forty Rules*, 44.

and restraint. It is formed by two different ideographs, making up the image of a double-bladed knife poised over the heart.

When the *ma* spaces in our lives become the deep voids of emptiness that seem to consume us, it is profoundly difficult to hold a posture of steadfast patient endurance. So perhaps practicing patience in the small spaces in daily life can strengthen us for the more enveloping and consuming chasms that can hold us in their grip. And practicing a receptivity to silence, stillness, and slowness can help us engage the *ma* spaces that we encounter, and receive the gifts of their essence. Such essence, like the aroma of paints and the aroma of Christ, can permeate us and mold us like clay, shaping into us that elusive deep quality of God we long to embody—patient endurance.

Icons as Theology and Prayer

The medieval icon painter Dionysius (1440–1502) is quoted by many as saying that the most essential part of iconography is the painter's own commitment to prayer. The iconographer is first to be a person who prays, and only second one who paints. When standing before an icon, the first significant thing to become aware of is the prayer that the Spirit prompts within oneself. The second thing of significance is to stay coupled in prayer with the Spirit and surrender to her movements within as she braids together heaven and earth, the infinite with the finite, the invisible with the visible, the spaces with meaning.

Kallistos Ware, the English bishop and theologian of the Eastern Orthodox Church, sees the Bible as a verbal icon of Christ, with the purpose of an icon being to reveal truth to humanity. Ware goes on to say that a person is "living theology" and is also an "icon of God."[18] Just as one does not worship the Bible, nor is the icon itself to be worshiped. It is the language of an icon that speaks to us of Ultimate Truth and Love. Theodore the Studite (759–826 CE) argued cogently against the iconoclasts of his time, clearly articulating that it was not the icon that was worshiped; rather, it was the One behind all created objects, including icons, who was the focus of adoration. It was not long after his death that icons were returned to Hagia Sophia in 843 CE. Much later, Hesychius (*circa* 1500s), abbot of the Mother of God Monastery in Sinai, is quoted in Ware's translation of the *Philokalia* as saying, "The Holy Gospel or New Testament is an icon of attentiveness, that is, of purity of heart."[19] And Gregory of Palamas (1296–1359 CE), who followed the hesychast life of a hermit, reminded his people, "You must not,

18. Ware, *Orthodox Church*, 214.
19. Ware, *Philokalia*, vol. 1, para. 112.

then, deify the icons of Christ and the saints, but through them you should venerate Him who created us in His own image, and who subsequently consented in His ineffable compassion to assume the human image and to be circumscribed by it."[20] And as we look into the face of another, we see the image of Christ there too. Each person we meet is an icon, made in the image of God. The icon's central purpose, whether it is the verbal icon of the Bible, the embodied icon of the neighbor next door, or the written icon on the wall, is always to reveal Truth, inspire through Love, point us to the Lord of All, prompt a praying spirit, and rouse us to action.

There are some general principles employed in iconography that also have theological and spiritual heuristic value. The first entails the apparent blank spaces or *ma* in icons, which are central to the whole experience of both writing and viewing an icon. In Byzantine painting, these spaces are deliberately devoid of any elements of perspective. This "background" represents the invisibility of God, including the absence of God, which is part of God's Presence. It is a space to ponder on, enter into, and allow the Spirit of God to speak through this "nothingness." Alexander Stoykov, in his remarkable treatise on the language of space in icons,[21] keeps reminding us that this apparently empty space is not simply a backdrop to the real action of the icon, but rather it is the alive environment of sacral light. Unlike negative space in art, which is often used to depict a certain shape, the space in icons has no spatial construction. I would suggest that to enter into such places is to enter into a visual form of the *via negativa* or apophatic way, which stresses God's unknowable transcendence. Through the immanence and accessibility of the icon's *ma* space, the apophatic or negative way is braided into transcendence and unknowability, where God's beyond-ness paradoxically sits within the same frame as God's visceral presence. The gold leaf of *Ma*, in its very different texture and quality, sets this space apart from the epiphanic liquids used in the spatial features of the icon.

An Alternate Perspective

Another iconographic principle is perspective. While not so evident in the *Vladimir* icon, most icons are drawn in such a way that instead of the lines converging on the horizon as in many forms of art, the lines converge in forefront. This scoops the viewer up into the scene of the icon, reminding the worshiper that they are not observers of the divine or of beauty, but

20. Ware, *Philokalia*, vol. 4, "A New Testament Decalogue," para. 6, Kindle location 21262.

21. Stoykov, *Language of Space*.

that they themselves embody and participate in divinity and beauty. This inverse perspective is enhanced by the way the light in an icon is portrayed. The light in an icon does not come from the sun, or from one particular source thereby creating shadows, but rather emanates from the icon as un-created light—the Light of God's self. This light, too, enfolds the worshiper into its embrace. The Jesuit Egon Sendler, a well-regarded expert on icons, describes this aspect of icons succinctly: the icon is "a place where a pres-ence is encountered. In the icon, the represented world shines out toward the person who opens himself to receive it. In inverse perspective, space itself becomes active instead of the observer who, in fact, is acted on."[22] In this way, icons may be seen as "living art," active and participating in the worshiper's spiritual journey.

Worth noting is that even though an iconographer seeks to represent to the best of their ability the original icon in every way, iconographers will attest to the remarkable way in which, without realizing it, the features of the faces will always be different, and at times in a mystical way seem to enfold in their facial lines something of the iconographer's own self. In this way too, we are drawn into the icon in more ways than we are aware of: not only the completed icon itself, but also in the process of writing an icon.

Other aspects of perspective specific to iconography include the por-trayal of buildings and structures from many sides at once, reflecting the all-seeing God who is outside time and space. And many times, Jesus is depicted in the arms of Mary with adult features when one would normally expect those of a baby, again inviting us to enter into a timelessness with the Divine. The multilayering of colors from dark to light and very light, includ-ing a mystical light, engages our awareness of the depths the Spirit of God's brush touches within us, painting us into the infinite depths of the Trinity.

A Further Look at the Vladimir Icon

Taking a deeper look at the *Vladimir* icon, more of the theology shines through, and the layering is there for each viewer to discover in the light of the Spirit. As we gaze through the icon, we are moved beyond the icon itself into the eyes, heart, arms—the very body and presence of God—through whom we are then opened to spiritual or religious insight. The eyes of the *Theotokos* are particularly engaging, where we see, among other things, the sorrow, compassion, love, and pathos as she embodies the celebration of the gift of Christ at the same time as experiencing the sword that is piercing her heart at the scourging and death that is also held in the icon. The love

22. Sendler, *Icon*, 127.

between the Mother and Child is alluring, where the two seem to form one shape, one body together. These elements are never exclusive, but rather include the worshiper in this divine love too. Rowan Williams, past Archbishop of Canterbury, reflects on this unity of love between them:

> Seizing handfuls of her clothing and nuzzling his face against hers, [Christ] shows us that God is not ashamed to be our God, to be identified as the one who is involved with us; here, though, it is as if he [Christ] is not merely unashamed but positively *shameless* in his eagerness, longing to embrace and be embraced. It is not simply that God will deign not to mind our company; rather he is passionate for it. The image of God's action we are presented with here is of a "hungry love."[23]

This chapter has looked at some of the *ma* spaces, which can challenge our assumptions of empty. It may be that the *ma* reveals an otherwise hidden essence that we hadn't noticed before. The space between branches is not something we can touch, yet it can invite us into the presence of the ineffable and transcendent God who fills all spaces. And the large areas of gold leaf with no detail in icons can entice us to move through the tangible golden space into the presence of the intangible God. *Ma* speaks to us through the language of breath and silent spaciousness, opening up a conversation with us, showing us how to see paradox through stereoscopic lenses, and ushering us through emptiness into discovering the fullness of possibilities.

23. Williams, *Ponder These Things*, 23.

7

God Comes to Us in Silence

A GREAT PILGRIMAGE
I felt in need of a great pilgrimage
so I sat still for three
days
and God came
to me.[1]

One doesn't need to go on huge expensive pilgrimages to encounter God. Kabir, the fifteenth-century Indian mystic, suggests the great pilgrimage is actually to be still. And God comes to us. When we become still, attentive, and seek silence right where we are, God comes as the voice of Love singing in our soul, and we discover God's voice and our voice becoming one. God comes singing to us in silence.

And yes, I thought I could hear her coming, humming as she padded along the deck to our front door. As a celebration, I had decided to invite friends from conversations with silence to afternoon tea. Passé the shadow, Grandmother God, Dragon Lizard, Susanna, Selah, and Ma. And

1 Kabir, quoted in Ladinsky, *Love Poems from God*, 227.

Grandmother God was arriving earlier than expected. I smiled as I got up to go to the door. She bustled in, giving me the most generous hug, with her multiple scarves and capes ballooning around me, enveloping me in the smell of sun-warmed dark plums and sparkling shiraz. I showed her the way to our sunroom, where the afternoon sun was lighting the room. She put down her tapestry bag and took off her cape, placing it across the back of the chair. I noticed under the cape she was wearing a layered skirt with swirling patterns of earthy colors reaching down to her feet, which were brown and rounded and bare. I smiled again. How good is this, I thought to myself.

The low coffee table had all but disappeared under the spread of freshly baked cupcakes, cucumber sandwiches (which I had rarely ever made), nuts and dates carefully arranged on the plates, wedges of cheeses and crackers laid out on a platter with strawberries and blueberries scattered between them. And last of all, a small plate of crunchy black ants for my friend Dragon Lizard, the only one with dietary requirements. I was filled with excitement. This was going to be such a special time with us all coming together.

"Tea? Coffee? Sparkling water?" I asked.

"Tea—definitely tea! A big pot of hot tea is just what I need," she said, following me into the kitchen.

I realized she belonged here as she automatically went to the fridge and pulled out the milk, pouring it into a jug she found in the cupboard. Waiting for the kettle to boil, we leaned against the counter and just gazed at each other, grinning. How good it was to be together again, and to have the moment to ourselves, just to be. So much said between us in this moment of silent gazing. The water was boiling, so I filled the teapot and took the tray through to the sunroom, just as the doorbell chimed. Who would this be?

Opening the door, I was standing in front of Passé. He had come in charcoal grey, with a gold sash across his chest, looking very dapper. What joy it was to see him, and as I turned and he followed me into the house, I felt a sense of déjà vu. A good sense. In the sunroom, he greeted Grandmother God with a deep bow, and sat next to her, shifting his shape to do so, and began asking her about her favorite blends of tea. I poured his cup just as there came a knock on the door.

It was Ma, splendidly arrayed as a wide picture frame of rich Huon pine, intricately carved with flowers and vines that looped out like many small arms. He looked so magnificent, and the pine grains and shades of yellow hues were remarkable. I felt a little intimidated, and wondered if my own simple outfit was enough for the occasion. But he seemed unconcerned, and greeted me so warmly I was immediately at ease. I ushered him through to meet the others and, since it was the first time they were meeting each other like this, I introduced them formally. But in a strange way, they seemed very comfortable with each other, as if they had met before. Ma found a good place near the coffee table where he propped his one-and-a-half square meter self against the wall, settling in as he began joking about the spaces between the chairs. Ma wanted some herbal tea, and so I headed back to the kitchen and found some sage tea at the back of the cupboard, making it in a small white two-cup pot for him. Before I could leave the kitchen, I saw someone arriving, and there on the deck were Selah and Susanna, who had met each other coming down the sandstone footpath.

They had stopped short of the door, deep in conversation about some-thing, but I was too impatient and raced out to meet them. Susanna leaned forward and gave me the most wonderful hug! And she handed me a brown paper bag. I carefully pulled the top of the bag open and peered inside: two pomegranates! I showed Selah, who immediately laughed and clapped her hands. I looked at her quizzically. Did she already know about this? I took them into the kitchen to put the fruit in a bowl, and found out they were both coffee drinkers, so set about making a steaming pot of percolated coffee.

Selah moved around the kitchen, peering at the few paintings that hung on the wall. She moved with such litheness. She reminded me of a light green-blue watercolor wash, almost like wisps of cloud; she was airy, and I couldn't quite figure out what sort of shape she was, but she reminded me most of a violin. And when she moved, I thought I could smell spearmint wafting past me.

Susanna had picked up the tray with coffee and milk and Ma's tea, and we went through to the sunroom. More greetings, and the coffee and tea flowed. Susanna had seated herself next to Passé, and they were already locked in conversation. It seemed as if whomever Susanna spoke with, they would immediately dive into something obviously engaging. I sat back with my cup of tea. Susanna was tall, and elegant, her floral pantaloons and cream jacket suited her so well, with dangling hibiscus earrings which only someone like her could wear. Her long dark hair was parted in the middle and braided down her back, and she had stretched out her long legs, which reached under the table.

I looked at my watch—Dragon Lizard had not yet arrived, and I was beginning to get worried. I handed around the plate of cupcakes. I hadn't as yet spoken much myself, but I felt so warmed by the buzz in the room. Connections were certainly happening. As I reached for the cheese and crackers, I saw a movement out of the corner of my eye, and turned to see Dragon Lizard had let himself in and had followed the noise! What a joy to see him! And he made a grand entrance, his noble head held high, his green coat tails splaying out over his long back, a crimson cravat around his neck, and he had painted his toenails just for the occasion. Bright red! He leapt nimbly onto the chair next to me, and held out his front foot to shake hands. I couldn't help but remark on his nails, and he simply gave a very broad grin, obviously pleased that we had all noticed. He handed me a spray of desert grasses: "For memory's sake; and they don't need much water!"

"Oh my goodness! This is perfect. Thank you. I will put these above the fireplace and I will so enjoy sharing my home with them." I kissed him warmly on the side of his head, and went off to find a clay pot to stand them in. I returned to the sunroom and, knowing what his drink of choice would be, I poured him a glass of sparkling water.

Well, we had all arrived. We were together. We were all looking around the circle—a circle of new friends with so much in common. Before I could speak, Grandmother God piped up.

"Dearest and blessed company, before we begin, I have brought a small gift for us." She reached down into her hag, and pulled out a palm-sized dark rock. "This," she said, holding it out for us all to see, "is a nugget of black granite, and as I am sure we will all have lots to talk about, I thought that instead of having a talking stick, we could have a talking stone."

I shook my head in wonder. This was echoing the granite Rosetta Stone! And I often finish a retreat I am facilitating by having the participants gather in a circle, often with some kind of "talking stick," where all may share something of their reflections and experiences. And here we were, at the end of an adventure into the landscapes of silence.

She continued, "So when you wish to speak, you hold the stone, and the rest of us will be listening. When you have finished, place the stone on the table, and then when someone else is ready to speak, they pick up the stone and hold it while they do so." She leaned forward to place the small rock on the table and, as she did so, her skirt shifted, and I noticed a tattoo along the arch on the inside of her foot.

I reached for the stone. "Well, I have a question," I began. "Would you like to tell us all about the tattoo on your foot?"

Everyone leaned forward to have a look, as Grandmother God held her foot out for us all to see.

"Holy ground," read Selah.

She smiled at our expectant faces. "Ah, there's a story," she said as she picked up the talking stone from where I had replaced it, and relaxed back deep into her chair.

Her eyes were dark and soft as she began. "I have found as I have wandered the earth, just how much my feet speak to me. As I walk across door thresholds that have broken glass and broken lives and broken dreams scattered underfoot, my soles speak to my soul, calling out that here too is holy ground." She rubbed her feet together, gently. "A sacred place where I will stand with them in wailing lament, holding their shaking bodies. I don't wear shoes, as I want to be with them with my own bareness and vulnerability. And, after however long is needed, when tears are spent and the silence of exhaustion follows, this silence becomes the holy ground of new sound. Previous images of love drop away, and a new Love is re-imaged and embraced. And right in this desert of pain, together we can find droplets of sweetness and honey, if those who are there will dig with me." She sipped some tea. "And so, I had 'Holy ground' inked onto my foot." Grandmother God rolled the stone around in her hand, feeling its texture, and seeing if there was anything more to say at this point. She then gently laid it on the table.

We all looked at the stone, a bit like the way one watches the flames of a fire in the fireplace. The rock didn't crackle, but it had its own form of silent presence.

Susanna sighed deeply. She picked up the stone and ran her finger over its surface, gazing at it intently. "And I also like the way you give space for long wailing to happen. When we hold that in, or can't voice our pain or our story, our throats close up, and we choke and can't breathe. That's what happened to me, and all that was left for me was to die."

Passé gently placed his hand on her arm. She took a deep breath and continued. "But our throats are birthing canals, giving birth to a voice that sounds out who we are; our sense of self is birthed, and healing of our silenced lives and the world's silenced stories can begin. It is as if a tourniquet is released and the lifeblood flows again, flushing with new life. So, voicing and protest is a sacred practice for all of us. And this way we can offer new ways of seeing the world and each other. Even those who have taken on the role of silencer can be released from their own distorted lenses, and slowly find a different vision."

Selah reflected, "Susanna, your experience reminds me of the psalmist's words, that out of the mouths of babes—those who are vulnerable and inarticulate—God brings strength.[2] And I hear you also saying that protests and street marches are sacred practices of voicing."

Susanna nodded.

Grandmother God leaned across and placed a finger on the stone. "Perhaps you could get a tattoo," she joked gently. "I can see it now: 'The Way of Life' tattooed sideways from the base of your throat to up under your chin!"

Susanna's face broke into a smile. "I would have to have my trusty tamarisk tree tattooed up my neck too! He's my totem." She slowly replaced the stone.

2. Ps 8:2.

In the ensuing silence, it felt as if Batach was here with us now too, and I thought, this time together is indeed a *temenos* time for us all. Another kind of holy ground with this company of witnesses. I am not a tattoo person myself, but I wondered if I were to ever get one, what would it say and where would I put it? And what might that say to those around me in its inked speech?

Dragon Lizard slid forward onto the table. He carefully rearranged his coattails, then placed his foot on the talking stone. And paused. Silent. He wasn't in a hurry. I found myself beholding him with such tenderness in all his unusual scaly beauty. His jaws were slowly moving in his habitual way, and the room had a deep stillness.

"It is good to be here," he began. His voice had a gentle gruffness to it, and as he spoke the scales around his head shone with a soft burnished kind of light. He spoke quietly, and I could see we were all leaning in toward him, listening intently. All leaning in to listen, I reflected. How interesting that Dragon Lizard has this effect: just as he drew me in to listen and to receive his gifts of wisdom in the desert, here too, he was drawing us all in. And as we did so, our attentiveness to everything about him was heightened, and it seemed we were all alert to the most miniscule of movement, of sound, and of silence coming from him. He was stock still. And so were we.

I don't know how long we sat in this dragon-lizard-silence, but it became a most wonderful, warm silence, with such a mellowing effect on us. He moved his hooded eyes to calmly rest on Grandmother God and, as I glanced at her, I could see they were exchanging a deep knowing. His eyes then slowly roved and rested upon each of us in turn. As his eyes held mine, my whole body felt held. The whole of him, with the whole of me. In the same way as when I first met him, he was again showing me through his silent, still body, what it meant to be wrapped in a sacred beholding that embraced so attentively and without judgment. And just as his body in the desert channelled the necessary scarce water droplets into his mouth for sustenance and life, so too I was learning from him that paying attention to my own body, in silence and stillness, channels the nourishment of calmness and perspective that is life-giving. He looked down at the stone under his foot. It looked to me like he smiled at the stone, before slowly taking his foot off it.

He looked across at Ma. "Can you catch?" Dragon Lizard asked.

"Of course," said Ma, as one of his carved-vine arms reached out and nimbly caught the talking stone lobbed to him.

"You obviously sensed I wanted to follow on from you," Ma gleamed at Dragon Lizard, who replied straight back, "Ah, but I have always been able to see right through you."

Dragon Lizard swayed with delight, while some of us groaned and Ma rolled his eyes. Then in the quiet that followed, Ma curled his vine arm slowly around towards his middle, holding the stone open on his palm in the midst of his Ma space. The black granite contrasted with the golden-yellow of the Huon pine wood of his hand, the smooth polished texture of the wood against the rough granite, the yellow against the black, the lumpiness of the small stone in the midst of the airy spaciousness encompassed by the splendidly carved frame. And Ma simply held it there. I gasped under my breath. A window of such beauty. I was reminded of the Aslan tree, where the openness between branches was anything but empty space. And the tenderness icon with its gold leaf, which had invited me right into its space, where I encountered the intimacy and "touchability" of the ineffable God. And now, here in this room, all of our silences were being invited through *this* icon, this door into the silent spaciousness of God.

Ma's voice was strong yet with a husky airiness and, as he spoke, the rainforest aroma that Huon is so famous for permeated the room like an incense of praise and presence. "The gift I would like to bring today, is just myself. Some people would say I am unfinished as I am, and need to be filled to be complete." There was a pause while I think we all recalled times when others had somehow implied that we were incomplete, or not enough, lacking in some way. "But I know in this company, you all understand me, and see me for who I really am. I like to offer the fullness of possibility through an open space where anyone can step in and become who they are being invited to be: the incarnate presence of Justice, Truth, and Love. Just as God was not afraid of the void, but stepped into it and, with the Spirit who hovered over the chaos, created all things, visible and invisible, so too each of us can put aside our fear of emptiness and instead step in and allow the Spirit to brood over us and awaken us and our world into an encounter with Love."

I couldn't take my eyes off the space framed by Ma. The dark stone on his hand in the middle took up such a small portion of the whole space. And yet it seemed so right, so balanced, and all the more beautiful for it. Ma slowly withdrew his hand with the stone from inside himself, and gave it to Selah to return it to the table. Selah hesitated, and instead held onto it. Selah looked at Ma.

"You and I have a lot in common, Ma," she said in her blue water-colored melodic voice. "While I open silent moments to enable hearing and listening into God, you open silent moments for looking and seeing into God. Our dialects have similar roots and the same longing," she observed. "I offer tiny houses of time and you offer tiny houses of space and even huge castles of space." She paused. "And our doors are always open," she said.

As I looked at her violin-like shape, I noticed that of course part of what makes the music emerge well is not only the type of wood used, but also the open space inside the violin. And spaces between the strings are also important for playing and sound quality. And here I was seeing the link that Selah was referring to: the physical spaces, along with the time spaces between musical notes, come together to offer a spaciousness of hospitality in which to encounter God, the One who always hosts the space. And the physical space between stanzas in a poem or psalm also allows Selah to offer her invitation of time to pause.

Selah looked across at Passé, and raised her eyebrow as if to ask whether he would like to say something. He hesitated for a moment, and changed position in his seat, not from discomfort, but it appeared he was somehow shifting into almost a viola shape as his eyes met with Selah's. "Thank you," he said as he leaned over to receive the stone. "Sorry but I just do this naturally. It's the way I am made. I always feel such an affinity with others, I just take on their shape automatically." He seemed a bit reticent and I wondered what he was feeling.

"I usually go near last or last at these things," he began. "Because I am so used to people preferring I didn't exist, or worse, pretending that I don't exist, let alone have something to offer. It is good to be among my own kin where we value each other. So thank you, *Selah*, for asking me. It has made me see that I have got into a habit I need to break, assuming you don't want to hear from me. But of course you all do! We are family here; our last name is Silence." Grandmother God chortled and poured a round of tea for those drinking it. Rather than sounding sorry for himself, Passé's reflection rather had a sadness to it, a realization that this attitude to shadow was so deeply embedded in many people, cultures, and institutions. He sat forward, with his left arm across his knee and his other hand holding the stone up under his chin, shape-shifting again to reflect Auguste Rodin's 1880 statue, *The Thinker*. His charcoal-colored self was in silhouette form, but it was obvious what he was portraying. We were gathered around him in our different forms of silence, just waiting until he was ready to speak.

There was a gravitas about him, the way he could hold such unaddressed darkness with such lightness of being. And his gold sash was a shiny satin with gold embroidery down the edges. Gold on gold. It was as if it was calling out to be noticed.

He continued reflectively, "I love accompanying all things, people in particular. I am a close companion and I know how to be attached without being demanding. I find it interesting that people fear me as much as they do. They fear the darkness as well as the gold." He looked over at Dragon Lizard. "You know what I'm talking about. You and I both have this effect on people when they encounter us. But we also know how good it is when instead of being repelled by us, they spend time with us and learn our language."

He lifted up the gold sash, took it off over his head and laid it across his knees. He smoothed it out, pondering its brightness and elegance. It was very beautiful and seemed to have a radiance about it.

"If I could wave a magic wand," he continued, as he sat back in his chair, "I would begin a new shadow play. But unlike the ancient shadow plays of the first millennium, where flat cutout puppets were played in such a way that their shadows were viewed through a screen, I would develop a new drama series. In my theatre plays there would be no screens and no puppets. I would have a group of people who would engage their silent shadows in conversations, and real stories could then be told of friendships developing between people and their dark shadows as well as their golden shadows. We could then move to drama involving institutions and even cultures dialoguing with their shadows. And stories of wondrous personal and spiritual transformation would be told. And perhaps the last series would be how scapegoats emerged from rejected shadows. And then," he said as he threw his hands gleefully in the air, "we would have a new generation of saints released to do wondrous good in the world!"

We all clapped at his speech.

"I might not seem very appealing," Passé said as he looked around the room, placing the stone back on the table. "Some think I am a bit too shady. But, oh, I am certainly worth getting to know!" He leaned back and stretched, then clasped his hands behind his head in a relaxedness that reflected us all.

We all found ourselves stretching. We had been sitting so still for some while. We got up and walked around, and I filled up the water jug. I knew it would soon be time to part.

As we gathered back in the sunroom, the sun was now low, and the dusk light was warm—the kind of light that makes faces glow. The time of day that the Zulus call *selibant'abahle*: the time of beautiful people. This was indeed that time.

We settled back, and I picked up the talking stone. I looked around at this wonderful company of witnesses to silence.

"Thank you all so much for coming. I have been anticipating this time together for so long. Being able to introduce you to each other, and have conversations about conversations with silence is indeed rich for me. And it has helped remind me of the things you have taught which are worth remembering and treasuring." I realized just how much I had come to love each one of these precious beings in the room. "I would like to share some other things that I have learned from each of you. And perhaps I can start with you, Passé." I turned to him.

"Passé, my dear friend, thank you for sticking with me through thick and thin. Through the times of my resistance and my slow realizations. It has been so good to walk with you. You show how distractions can in fact be messages from you, my dark shadow, and that with silence as a conversation partner through you, a poultice can be placed on my woundedness, and the toxins brought to the surface. Thank you. And I look forward to talking more with you, but next time, maybe it could be about the golden shadow?" He nodded in delight.

I looked across at Grandmother God. "You continue to give new ways of seeing and being with you, God. Images and metaphors that give life. Oh, and I will never forget the honeypot ants! How can I ever thank you enough?"

She slapped her hands on her thighs and laughed, "Well, we also have eternity together to enjoy that!"

I said, "The desert can bring us to the brink of an internal abyss, but then also it can sweep us up into experiencing the exquisiteness of the land-scape and the skies. It can be a roller-coaster ride. But your constancy, felt and unfelt, keeps us going."

Placing the stone in my lap, I took the foot of Dragon Lizard in my hands. "Your gift of the scratchy, pointed grasses is exactly the gift I need!" Dragon Lizard grinned broadly, and his tail flicked a salute. "You know I thought they were terribly coarse and uninviting, and also that I thought you were, well, plain ugly! But look what a great teacher you have been! Meister Eckhart said, "God is in all things as being, as activity, as power. . . . [E]very creature is a vestige of God" (sermon 2).[3] It's as though every creature and every plant is a word from God and a book about God. You speak of God through your stillness, attentiveness, and silence.

"Susanna, thank you for letting me join voices with you, joining all the other voices that break unhealthy silences. Your prayer reminds us all just how powerful prayer is. You continue to be such a wise companion for those who have experienced power imbalances and abuse. And midrash helps us step into the silent spaces in the text where your voiced story should have been, and where those captured and imprisoned by such structures can be given a chance to be heard." Susanna nodded her head in acknowledgment, her earrings jangling. At this point, I reached into my pocket and pulled out a small package wrapped in crimson paper with a thin white ribbon.

3. Eckhart, *Seven Sermons*, Pf2, Q102,QT58.

"Susanna, I want to give you these as a gift. As I give it to you, it is also a gift to all who have walked in your shoes. I would love you to have these."

She reached out and took the parcel somewhat shyly. "Shall I open it now?" she asked.

The chorus of "Yes!" went up from others in the room. She carefully undid the ribbon and put it aside, then unwrapped the crimson tissue paper. Out fell two earrings. They were two small green cocoons, each with a series of gold dots around the middle. She held them up for all to see. They really were fine and quite delicately made.

"*Recherché!*" exclaimed Susanna. "This really calls for celebration," she said, as she got up and did a quick shuffle dance that made us all whoop and clap with her. She sat back down and took out her hibiscus earrings, and carefully replaced them with the dangling green cocoons. They suited her absolutely.

Grandmother God leaned over and said in a theater whisper, "Now all you need is that tattoo we talked about!"

This really was a great celebration! We all toasted Susanna with glasses of water, with cries of "*Recherché!*"

"Oh, I almost forgot," I interjected. "Thank you for being such a role model in spending time developing a special *temenos*. It reminds us all to take the time to do that, to listen to the trees, and to draw deeply into the silence of God in nature."

Susanna sat down at last, and looking across at me she looked deeply into me and mouthed, "Thank you!"

I stood up and went over to Ma. Now such a familiar and close friend. "Ma, you opened a whole world up to me. What I thought were simply empty, non-functional spaces . . ."

"With no objectives or outcomes," he interjected with a knowing smile.

"Indeed!" I chuckled. "But wow, what you open up for us is a universe to be explored. All the spaces in architecture, nature, art, gardens . . . it's all there. Places where we can be slowed down to notice that nothing is never simply nothing. That all spaces have invitations, and we can step inside and discover worlds of possibilities. Even the spaces in the process of iconography—or any painting for that matter—between the brush and the paper, the colors, the so-called negative spaces, all invite us to notice something new."

"Absolutely!" cried Ma, clapping his vine-carved hands. "And now, I have . . . nothing . . . more to add!"

As I turned to Selah, the last of all, she got up and came and sat on my lap, draping her arm around my neck, and planting a great kiss on my cheek. Everyone laughed. She was so good at draping herself; her colors washed over me and her spearmint scent was delightfully fresh. She was so light and airy; I couldn't tell quite whether she was sitting on me or I was somehow inside her . . . just like being inside a not-so-tiny house of wispy time. The way she made herself at home on my lap reminded me not of a violin now, but more of a cat, lithe and light and comical. This was a side of Selah I hadn't seen before, and we were all enjoying it.

I found it difficult to be serious with her arrayed over me (or was she encompassing me?), but I did my best. "Selah, you stopped me in my tracks, and gave me the most wonderful gift of a tiny silent space that opened up into a cavern larger than you can imagine. And that's what you do for all of us. You offer those moments to pause, reflect, and open up a stairwell for us to go down into the place where God is waiting to do deep work." Was she purring? I chose to ignore it and carried on. "One of your gifts to the world is the pauses between words, the psalms, poetry, and also the silences between, before, and after notes and all music. In fact, you show us how your silence is the ground of all sound."

Then I spoke to everyone. "Most of all, I want to say, I would never have met any of you if I had not taken the opportunity to learn the language of silence and the soul through the Rosetta Stone of attentiveness and still-ness." I held up the black granite stone that Grandmother God had gifted the gathering. "This has been our Rosetta Stone for the afternoon, our talking stone, facilitating the conversations between each of our silences." I handed the stone to Selah who was still on my lap. "And lastly, to know that learning any language cannot be separated from relationship is a most treasured wisdom. Each of you embodies the God who comes to us in and through silence, and always comes in service of healing and wholeness. Thank you for coming today."

At this point, Selah began to sound a note that was high, but not at all piercing. It was like satin threads silking through the air. Grandmother God joined in. And we all began to stand up and together joined in with our own note that came from deep within us, a note that expressed who we were. For some it came as a deep hum, for others a wide-mouthed "Aaah." It was a beautiful, ethereal sound, joining all our silences together. We were standing close together forming a circle and, as the sound dropped away, we stood still, a company of witnesses, in the late afternoon sun.

As we have traversed the landscapes of silence, our quest has been to engage *with* silence, to learn to hear and speak that language of silence, what John of the Cross referred to as the first language of God. My hope is that by coming on this pilgrimage you will have found this book to be an accessible companion as a gateway into fresh encounters with the language of God. And whatever your previous experiences of silence may have been, may you find yourself now learning the language anew.

Conversations with Silence reminds us that the Rosetta Stone of the soul is not some relic kept far away and unavailable in the British Museum, but like the original stela, which was placed in the midst of the market square for all to read, so too this Rosetta Stone is in our midst. The small black granite talking stone now lies on your table in your home. The invitation is there for you should you wish to pick it up and hold it when you have a moment of stillness and silence and, as you do, you may find yourself not only hearing the sound of silence, but speaking it.

Bibliography

Alexander, Philip. *The Mystical Texts: Songs of the Sabbath Sacrifice and Related Manuscripts*. London: T. & T. Clark, 2006.

Appleton, George, ed. *The Oxford Book of Prayer*. New York: Oxford University Press, 1986.

Bal, Mieke. *Anti-Covenant: Counter-Reading Women's Lives in the Hebrew Bible*. Sheffield, UK: Sheffield Academic Press, 2009.

Bennett, Stephanie. "Endangered Habitat: Why the Soul Needs Silence." *Ploughing Quarterly* Winter (2018) 66–69.

Binz, Stephen J. *Transformed by God's Word: Discovering the Power of Lectio and Visio Divina*. Notre Dame, IN: Ave Maria, 2016.

Bird, Michael. *Jesus and the Origins of the Gentile Mission*. London: Continuum, 2007.

Bloom, Anthony. *Beginning to Pray*. New York: Paulist, 1970.

Blue, Lilly. "Poetry as a Way of Seeing: Risk, Silence and Attention." *Literacy Learning: The Middle Years* 24 (2016) 26–33.

Bly, Robert, trans. *Kabir: Ecstatic Poems*. Boston: Beacon, 2007.

Boden, Alison L. *In the Hand of God*. Nov 1, 2015. https://chapel.princeton.edu/news/hand-god.

Bourgeault, Cynthia. *Centering Prayer and Inner Awakening*. Cambridge, MA: Cowley, 2004.

Bouteneff, Peter C. *Arvo Pärt: Out of Silence*. New York: St. Vladimir's Seminary Press, 2015. Kindle edition.

Breitman, Barbara Eve. "Spiritual Transformation: A Psychospiritual Perspective on Jewish Narratives of Journey." In *Jewish Spiritual Direction: An Innovative Guide from Traditional and Contemporary Sources*, edited by Howard Avruhm Addison and Barbara Eve Breitman. Nashville: Jewish Lights, 2006. Kindle edition.

Brueggemann, Walter. "The Liturgy of Abundance, the Myth of Scarcity." *Christian Century* 24 (1999). https://www.christiancentury.org/article/2012–01/liturgy-abundance-myth-scarcity.

Carson, Anne. "Putting Her in Her Place: Women, Dirt, and Desire." In *Before Sexuality: The Construction of Erotic Experience in the Ancient Greek World*, edited by David M. Halperin, John J. Winkler, and Froma I. Zeitlin, 135–69. Princeton, NJ: Princeton University Press, 1990.

Casey, Michael. *Sacred Reading: The Ancient Art of Lectio Divina*. Chicago: Triumph, 1996.

Chadwick, Henry, trans. *Confessions by Saint Augustine*. Oxford: Oxford University Press, 1991.

Chesterton, G. K. *Orthodoxy*. London: Bodley Head, 1908.

Chittister, Joan. *In Search of Belief*. Liguori, MO: Liguori/Triumph, 2006.

Chryssavgis, John. *In the Heart of the Desert: Spirituality of the Desert Fathers and Mothers*. Bloomington, IN: World Wisdom, 2008. Kindle edition.

Claassens, L. Juliana M. *Claiming Her Dignity: Female Resistance in the Old Testament*. Collegeville, MN: Liturgical, 2016. http://ebookcentral.proquest.com.

Curzon, David. *Modern Poems on the Bible: An Anthology*. Philadelphia: Jewish Publication Society, 1994.

de Caussade, Jean-Pierre. *Abandonment to Divine Providence: Including "Spiritual Counsels of Père de Caussade" and "Letters on the Practice of Abandonment."* Floyd, VA: Wilder, 2014. Kindle edition.

———. *The Sacrament of the Present Moment*. Glasgow: Collins, 1966.

de Mello, Anthony. *The Way to Love: The Last Meditations of Anthony de Mello*. New York: Doubleday, 1995.

de Saint-Exupéry, Antoine. *Wind Sand and Stars*. New York: Harcourt Brace Javanovich, 1967. https://www.wesjones.com/wind%20sand%20stars/wind%20sand%20stars%20-%2009%20-%20barcelona%20and%20madrid%20(1936).xml.

de Saint-Exupéry, Antoine, and Richard Howard. *The Little Prince*. Boston: HMH Books for Young Readers, 2000.

Downey, Michael. *The Depth of God's Reach: A Spirituality of Christ's Descent*. Maryknoll, NY: Orbis, 2018. Kindle edition.

Easwaran, E. *Conquest of Mind: Take Charge of Your Thoughts and Reshape Your Life through Meditation*. Tomales, CA: Blue Mountain Center of Meditation, 2010.

Eckhart, Meister. *Seven Sermons*. Scotts Valley, CA: CreateSpace, 2009.

Elder, E. V. *Embracing the Spirit Within*. Victoria, BC: Friesen, 2012.

Endean, Philip. "Discerning behind the Rules: Ignatius' First Letter to Teresa Rejadell." *The Way* 64 (1989) 37–50.

Exum, J. Cheryl. "Fragmented Women: Feminist (Sub)Versions of Biblical Narratives." *Journal for the Study of the Old Testament* Supplement 163 (1993) 170–201.

Fischer, Kathleen. *Women at the Well*. New York: Paulist, 1988.

Fitzgerald, Constance. "Carmelite Beatitudes: Homily for Sister Agnes Kyungee of Jesus' First Profession." 2007. http://www.carmelite.org/documents/Spirituality/fitzgeraldcarmelitebeatitudes.pdf.

———. "From Impasse to Prophetic Hope: Crisis of Memory." *CTSA Proceedings* 64 (2009) 21–42.

Fiumara, Gemma Corradi. *The Other Side of Language: A Philosophy of Listening*. Translated by C. Lambert. London: Routledge, Chapman & Hall, 1990.

Fletcher, Alan. *The Art of Looking Sideways*. New York: Phaidon, 2001.

Fox, Matthew. *Hildegard of Bingen: A Saint for Our Times*. Vancouver: Namaste, 2012.

———. *A Spirituality Named Compassion and the Healing of the Global Village: Humpty Dumpty and Us*. Minneapolis: Winston, 1979.

Frankel, Estelle. *Sacred Therapy*. Berkeley: Shambhala, 2005. Kindle edition.

Gallagher, Timothy M. *Discernment of Spirits: An Ignatian Guide for Everyday Living*. New York: Crossroad, 2005.

————. *The Examen: Ignatian Wisdom for Our Lives Today.* New York: Crossroad, 2006.

Garcia-Rivera, Alex. *A Wounded Innocence: Sketches for a Theology of Art.* Collegeville, MN: Liturgical, 2003.

Gehman, Henry Snyder, ed. *The New Westminster Dictionary of the Bible.* Philadelphia: Westminster, 1970.

Glancy, Jennifer. "The Accused: Susanna and Her Readers." *Journal for the Study of the Old Testament* 58 (1993) 103–16.

Goldsworthy, Anna. *Piano Lessons: A Memoir.* New York: St. Martin's, 2013.

Guite, Malcolm. *Faith, Hope and Poetry: Theology and the Poetic Imagination.* Farnham, UK: Ashgate, 2012.

Hales, Christine Simoneau. *Eyes of Fire: How Icons Saved My Life as an Artist.* Independently published, 2018. Kindle edition.

Hammer, Jill. *Sisters at Sinai: New Tales of Biblical Women.* Philadelphia: Jewish Publication Society, 2001.

Hanvey, James. "The Leaden Echo and the Golden Echo: Hopkins's Vision of a Christian Ethic." *The Way* Supplement 66 (1989) 52–67.

Hawes, Patrick. Email exchange. April 25, 2019.

Hildegard of Bingen. *The Letters of Hildegaard of Bingen: Volume II.* Translated by Joseph L. Baird and Radd K. Ehrman. Oxford: Oxford University Press, 1998.

Holmes, Barbara. *Joy Unspeakable.* Pennsylvania: Fortress, 2017.

Hopkins, G. M. *Gerard Manley Hopkins: Complete Poems.* Long Beach, CA: Lexicos, 2012. Kindle edition.

Ignatius of Loyola. *The Spiritual Exercises of St. Ignatius.* Scotts Valley, CA: CreateSpace, 2017.

Jeanrond, Werner. "Love and Silence." *Concilium,* Silence (2015) 13–21.

Johnson, Robert A. *Owning Your Own Shadow: Understanding the Dark Side of the Psyche.* New York: HarperOne, 1991. Kindle edition.

Johnston, William. *Mystical Theology: The Science of Love.* Maryknoll, NY: Orbis, 1998.

Jordan, P. J., and C. Chang. "Penetration of Private Places in Theodotian Susanna." *HTS Teologiese Studies/Theological Studies* 74 (2018) 1–8. https://doi.org/10.4102/hts.v74i3.5004.

Julian of Norwich. *Revelations of Divine Love.* Long Island: Ixia, 2019.

Kafka, Franz. *Letters to Friends, Family, and Editors.* New York: Schocken, 1977.

Karchmar, Irving. "Darvish." March 16, 2013. https://darvish.wordpress.com/tag/rumi-poetry/.

Katz-Chernin, Elena. "Blue Silence." 2018. https://www.abc.net.au/rn/features/silence/blue/.

Kavanagh, Patrick. *Collected Poems.* Edited by Antoinette Quinn. London: Allen Lane, 2004.

Keefe-Perry, L. Callid. *Way to Water: A Theopoetics Primer.* Eugene, OR: Cascade, 2014.

Kelsey, Morton T. *The Other Side of Silence: A Guide to Christian Meditation.* New York: Paulist, 1976.

Kimmerer, Robin Wall. *Braiding Sweet Grass.* Minneapolis: Milkweed, 2013.

Kononenko, Igor. *Teachers of Wisdom.* Pittsburgh, PA: RoseDog, 2010.

Korzybski, Alfred. *Selections from Science and Sanity.* Edited by Lance Strate. New York: Institute of General Semantics, 2010.

Koslowski, Jutta. "Mother I Hear Your Heartbeat: Silence as Listening to God and His Creation." *Concilium* 5 (2015) 96–103.

Ladinsky, Daniel James. *Love Poems from God: Twelve Sacred Voices from the East and West*. New York: Penguin Compass, 2002.

Laird, M. S. *Into the Silent Land: A Guide to the Christian Practice of Contemplation*. Oxford: Oxford University Press, 2006.

———. *An Ocean of Light: Contemplation, Transformation, and Liberation*. Oxford: Oxford University Press, 2018.

———. *A Sunlit Absence: Silence, Awareness, and Contemplation*. New York: Oxford University Press, 2011. http://public.eblib.com/choice/publicfullrecord.aspx?p=72 8787.

Lanzetta, Beverly. *Radical Wisdom: A Feminist Mystical Theology*. Minneapolis: Fortress, 2005.

Levine, Amy-Jill. "Hemmed in on Every Side: Jews and Women in the Book of Susanna." In *A Feminist Companion to Esther, Judith, and Susanna*, edited by Athalya Brenner-Idan, 175–90. Sheffield, UK: JSOT, 1995.

Lewis, C. S. *The Lion, the Witch and the Wardrobe*. New York: Collier, 1970.

Lindbergh, Anne Morrow. *Gift from the Sea*. New York: Pantheon, 1955.

Lonegan, Bernard. *Insight: A Study of Human Understanding*. 1957. Reprint, Toronto: University of Toronto Press, 1997.

Longley, Sally. "Patience and the Art of Nurturing a Contemplative Posture as Spiritual Directors." *Presence: An International Journal of Spiritual Direction* 33 (2017) 49–54.

MacCulloch, Diarmaid. *Silence: A Christian History*. New York: Penguin, 2013.

Manser, Lynda. *Speak the Truth in a Million Voices—It Is Silence That Kills: Stories for Change*. Ottawa, ON: National Youth in Care Network, 2004.

Marx, Dalia. "The Prayer of Susanna (Daniel 13)." In *Ancient Jewish Prayers and Emotions Associated with Jewish Prayer in and around the Second Temple Period*, edited by Stephan Reif and Renate Egger-Wenzel, 221–36. Berlin: de Gruyter, 2015.

McCarty, V. K. "Renewing the Life that Brings Salvation: Theodore the Studite's Defense of Icon Veneration." Academa, General Seminary, 2019. https://www.academia. edu/38620721/Renewing_the_Life_that_Brings_Salvation_Theodore_the_ Studites_Defense_of_Icon_Veneration_by_V.K._McCarty.

McGuire, Philip C. *Speechless Dialect: Shakespeare's Open Silences*. Berkeley: University of California Press, 1985.

Merton, Thomas. *Thomas Merton's Gethsemane: Landscapes of Paradise*. Lexington, KY: University of Kentucky Press, 2005.

Merton, Thomas, and Jonathan Montaldo. *Entering the Silence: Becoming a Monk and Writer*. The Journals of Thomas Merton, vol. 2. San Francisco: HarperSanFrancisco, 1995. http://catdir.loc.gov/catdir/description/hc044/95030457.html.

Middleton, Andrew, and Dietrich Klemm. "The Geology of the Rosetta Stone." *Journal of Egyptian Archaeology* 89 (2003) 207–16. www.jstor.org/stable/3822498.

Mill, John Stuart. *On Liberty*. 1959. https://www.utilitarianism.com/ol/three.html.

Mirikitani, Janice. *Breaking Silence: Out of the Dust*. Los Angeles: UCLA Asian American Studies Centre, 2014.

Ni Riain, Noirin. *Theosophy: Towards a Theology of Listening*. Dublin: Columba, 2011.

Nitschke, G. "Ma—The Japanese Sense of Place." *Architectural Design, London*. 1966. https://kyotojournal.org/culture-arts/ma-place-space-void/.

Nouwen, Henri J. M. *The Return of the Prodigal Son: A Story of Homecoming*. London: Darton, Longman & Todd, 1984.

———. *The Way of the Heart: A Spirituality of the Desert Mothers and Fathers*. San Francisco: Harper One, 2016. Kindle edition.

Obbard, Elizabeth Ruth. *Through Julian's Window: Growing into Wholeness with Julian of Norwich*. Norwich, UK: Canterbury, 2008.

O'Connor, Elizabeth. *Search for Silence*. San Diego: LuraMedia, 1986.

Ouspensky, Léonide, and Vladimir Lossky. *The Meaning of Icons*. 2nd ed. Crestwood, NY: St. Vladimir's Seminary Press, 1982.

Painadath, Sebastian. "The Transforming Power of Contemplative Silence." *Concilium*, Silence (2015) 33–43.

Picard, Max. *The World of Silence*. Humanist Library. Chicago: Regnery, 1952.

Pope Francis. Encyclical letter *"Laudato Si'"* of the Holy Father Francis on Care for Our Common Home. Rome: The Vatican, 2015. http://www.vatican.va/content/francesco/en/encyclicals/documents/papa-francesco_20150524_enciclica-laudato-si.html.

Prestige, G. L. *The Life of Charles Gore*. London: Heinemann, 1935.

Priests for Equality. *The Inclusive Bible: The First Egalitarian Translation*. Lanham, MD: Rowman & Littlefield. 2007.

Rees, Elizabeth. *Early Christianity in South-West Britain: Wessex, Somerset, Devon, Cornwall and the Channel Islands*. Oxford: Oxbow, 2020.

Richards, Lawrence O. *The Global Concise Bible Dictionary*. Toronto: Global Christian, 1999.

Rohr, Richard. *Everything Belongs: The Gift of Contemplative Prayer*. New York: Crossroad, 2003.

———. "Struggling with Shadow." September 11, 2017. https://cac.org/struggling-with-shadow-2017-09-11/.

Ross, Maggie. *Silence: A User's Guide, Volume Two: Application*. Oregon: Cascade, 2017.

Rotenberg, Mordechai. *Psychology of Tzimtzum: Self, Other, and God*. No loc.: Maggid, 2016.

Rumi, Jalal Al-din. *Love's Ripening: Rumi on the Heart's Journey*. Boston: Shambhala, 2008.

Sakharov, Nicholas V. *I Love Therefore I Am: The Theological Legacy of Archmandrite Sophrony*. Crestwood, NY: St. Vladimir's Seminary Press, 2002. Kindle edition.

Sendler, Egon. *The Icon: Image of the Invisible*. Catrine, UK: Oakwood, 1996.

Shafak, Elif. *The Forty Rules of Love: A Novel of Rumi*. New York: Penguin, 2011.

Smart, Carol. *Feminism and the Power of Law*. London: Routledge, 1989.

Stein, Robert H. *An Introduction to the Parables of Jesus*. Philadelphia, Westminster, 1981.

Stoykov, Alexander. *The Language of Space in Byzantine Iconography*. New York: A. and A. Communications, 2014.

Stramara, Daniel F., Jr. "The Kolpos of the Father (Jn. 1:18) as the Womb of God in the Greek Tradition." *Magistra: A Journal of Women's Spirituality in History* 22.2 (2016) 36–53.

Tagore, Rabindranath. *Collected Poems and Plays of Rabindranath Tagore*. London: Macmillan, 1973.

Teasdale, Wayne. *The Mystic Heart: Discovering a Universal Spirituality in the World's Religions*. Novato, CA: New World Library, 2001.

Teilhard de Jardin, Pierre. "Patient Trust." In *Hearts on Fire: Praying with Jesuits*, edited by Michael Harter, 102–3. St. Louis, MO: Institute of Jesuit Resources, 1993.

Toner, Jules J. *A Commentary on Saint Ignatius' Rules for Discernment of Spirits: A Guide to the Principles and Practice*. St. Louis, MO: Institute of Jesuit Sources, 1982.

Trible, Phyllis. *Texts of Terror: Literary-Feminist Readings of Biblical Narratives*. Philadelphia: Fortress, 1984.

Uhlein, G. *Meditations with Hildegard of Bingen*. Santa Fe: Terra Nova, 1982.

Upjohn, Sheila. *Why Julian Now? A Voyage of Discovery*. Grand Rapids: Eerdmans, 1997.

Van Zuiden, Mirjam, et al. "Intranasal Oxytocin to Prevent Posttraumatic Stress Disorder Symptoms: A Randomized Controlled Trial in Emergency Department Patients." *Biological Psychiatry* 81 (2017), 1030–40.

Ward, Benedicta. *The Sayings of the Desert Fathers*. London: Mowbray, 1975.

Ware, Timothy, ed. *The Art of Prayer: An Orthodox Anthology*. London: Faber & Faber, 1966.

———. *The Orthodox Church: An Introduction to Eastern Christianity*. 3rd ed. London: Penguin, 2015.

———, trans. *The Philokalia*. Edited by St. Nikodimos of the Holy Mountain and St. Makarios of Corinth. Toronto. Kindle edition. https://archive.org/publish ingtoronto@gmail.com.

Weil, Simone. *Gravity and Grace*. London: Routledge, 2002.

West, Gerald, and Phumzile Zondi-Mabizela. "The Bible Story that Became a Campaign: The Tamar Campaign in South Africa (and Beyond)." *Ministerial Formation* 103 (2004) 4–12.

Wiener, Shohama Harris. "Spiritual Types: One Size Doesn't Fit All." In *Jewish Spiritual Direction: An Innovative Guide from Traditional and Contemporary Sources*, edited by Howard Avruhum Addison and Barbara Eve Breitman, Kindle loc 2460–2727. Nashville: Turner, 2006. Kindle edition.

Williams, Monty. *Stepping into Mystery: A Guide to Discernment*. Ottawa, ON: Novalis, 2012.

Williams, Rowan. *Ponder These Things: Praying with Icons of the Virgin*. Brewster, MA: Paraclete, 2006.

Wolters, C., ed. *The Cloud of Unknowing in Modern English*. London: Penguin Classics, 1961.

Zweig, Connie. *Meeting the Shadow of Spirituality: The Hidden Power of Darkness on the Path*. Bloomington, IN: iUniverse, 2017. Kindle edition.